Unless Recalled Earlier
Date Due

DEC 5 1990			

Oil-Futures
Markets

Oil-Futures Markets

An Introduction

William G. Prast
Howard L. Lax
Atlantis, Inc.

LexingtonBooks

D.C. Heath and Company
Lexington, Massachusetts
Toronto

Library of Congress Cataloging in Publication Data
Prast, William G.
   Oil-futures markets.

   Includes index.
   1. Petroleum industry and trade. 2. Commodity exchanges. I. Lax,
Howard L. II. Title.
HG6047.P47P7 1983   332.64'4   82-48622
   ISBM 0-669-06354-1

Copyright © 1983 by D.C. Heath and Company

Published simultaneously in Canada

Printed in the United States of America

International Standard Book Number: 0-669-06354-1

Library of Congress Catalog Card Number: 82-48622

Contents

Figures and Tables

Preface

Oil-futures trading is an idea whose time has come at last. Commodity traders with many years of experience in metals or agricultural products are now seeking to become familiar with the ways of the world petroleum industry. In addition, veteran oilmen are learning the ins and outs of the commodities-trading business.

This book provides a bridge between both parties. It assumes some, but not a lot of, knowledge on the part of the reader and is designed to introduce the theory and practice of oil-futures trading to a wide audience.

We at Atlantis have enjoyed putting this volume together and are indebted to many people in the United States and the United Kingdom for their unselfish help and encouragement. Any errors of fact are ours. Any differences of opinion are open to discussion, and we would be delighted to hear from you.

Part I
Commodity-Futures Markets

1

Functions of the Futures Market

Development of Futures Trading

The trading of commodity-futures contracts is unique. This specialized system of commerce came about because commodity dealers and users needed a system to permit the orderly operation of their businesses. Futures trading exists for a wide variety of products, ranging from egg and broiler-chicken contracts, to the more glamorous contracts for gold and silver. This book deals with a commodity that is one of the most recent to be traded in the futures markets: oil. In introducing the reader to petroleum futures, we have rooted this book in the functioning of both the international oil industry and world futures markets.

In this general introduction to the futures marketplace we will discuss the specifics of futures trading in petroleum products. How it differs from the general characteristics of futures trading will be discussed in part 3.

To put commodity-futures trading in perspective, it is important to remember that the usual function of the markets are to transfer ownership, but that this does not often happen in a futures market. Instead, futures markets exist chiefly to make it simple· to own contracts. Making and offsetting of those contracts is misleadingly called buying and selling and is only a side issue.

Futures contracts can be and are used chiefly as financial instruments, not as merchandising contracts. If dealing in these contracts was better labeled than by the phrase *buying and selling,* ordinary citizens would not be at all surprised to know that the transfer of ownership only occurs rarely.

It is often mistakenly thought that futures contracts came about as vehicles for speculative trading in forward contracts (contracts for deferred delivery). Although futures contracts would not have developed without the prior existence of forward contracts, the two exist as complements to one another, each serving a specific purpose. Forward contracts are merchandising agreements that explicitly defer the actual delivery of a commodity, whereas futures contracts are temporary substitutes for eventual merchandising contracts. Only about three percent of all futures contracts are settled by the physical delivery to the purchaser of a commodity, while forward contracts, by definition, culminate in the delivery of a product.

Commodity-exchange markets such as the London Metal Exchange began as ways to provide centralized marketplaces where buyers and sellers could meet, negotiate prices, and make deals. As worldwide trade grew and industry became more complex, the need arose for forward merchandising contracts that allow businessmen to plan ahead. As technology improved and control over product quality and consistency increased, standardized forward contracts— the foundation of futures contracts—developed for easy and efficient commodity trading. Standard contracts also prompted speculative trade, but this was a side effect. Standards were set at the behest of commodity handlers, to allow for greater business efficiencies by providing a common currency for trading.

Today, however, most of the merchandising trade that once took place on commodity exchanges has shifted from these centralized marketplaces. There are four major factors behind this move.

1. High-speed communications technology has eliminated the need for buyers and sellers to meet at one spot to negotiate prices.
2. As trade became concentrated in the hands of a relatively small number of large firms, the number of persons in the price-forming process—previously carried out in the open marketplace—diminished. One-to-one negotiations became a rarity, and trading firms came to represent many individual buyers and sellers.
3. The purpose of an open market is to arrive, through the workings of supply and demand, at a single price based on competitive bidding. This function of the market was obviated by more complex pricing systems and price-escalation terms in contracts.
4. The existence of futures trading in completely standardized forward contracts on most of the exchanges utilizes all available market information and further encourages merchandising contracts outside of the exchange. Merchandising contracts are not any less necessary because of futures trading but no longer benefit from negotiation at a central open market.

With merchandise trade handled privately, the trading of futures contracts became the sole activity of various commodities exchanges. To stay in business, exchanges developed new lines to attract new customers. One result has been that most exchanges introduced futures contracts in commodities that had not previously been traded in that manner. Aluminum on the London Metal Exchange is an example. This action by the commodities exchanges coincided with the need for a new price-formation process of bids and offers. Competitiveness having been seriously eroded by the withdrawal of the merchandising trade, a mechanism was required for more sensitive pricing information.

Rather than being fueled by speculation in forward contracts, the now matured system of trading in commodity-futures contracts depends primarily on those whose businesses are intimately tied to the commodities themselves. The standardization and consequent transferability of futures contracts has led to some speculation, which provides liquidity that is vital to the smooth functioning of the futures markets. Most participants in futures markets, however, are not speculators with no interest in the commodity being traded.

Function of Futures Markets

The primary purpose of the commodity-futures trade is to promote the continuous and orderly operation of those businesses that utilize wholesale quantities of certain basic materials. This is done through the use of specialized contracts. In fact, futures trading in some commodities did not survive in the past because it failed to attract a sufficient amount of trading by handlers of those commodities. Earlier efforts at establishing a futures trade in petroleum products failed for this reason. This fate may again befall the oil futures markets, though it is too early to tell, or even to make a preliminary judgement.

The commodity-futures trading functions because of the standardization of commodity-futures contracts. This standardization is applied to the four basic terms of a futures contract: the quantity of the product, the grade or quality, the place of delivery, and the date by which delivery must be made. Futures contracts are denoted by the month in which delivery is to be made. The seller, or buyer in some contracts, has the option of choosing the exact date in that month for delivery. For some commodities, contracts can be traded for delivery up to two years in the future. Because basic terms, other than the date of delivery, remain the same, these contracts are easily transferable and are freely traded. It is simple to enter into, and withdraw from, a futures contract.

By being party to such an agreement, an individual agrees either to make delivery, or to accept delivery, by a fixed date, at a fixed price, of a fixed amount of a standard grade of a commodity. To free himself from such a contract, the individual need merely offset his obligation by establishing a trading position equal to his original one. Thus, if a person enters into a contract whereby he agrees to buy one hundred tons of gas oil, he can free himself from this obligation by entering into an offsetting contract whereby he agrees to sell one hundred tons of a similar gas oil. The ease of trading is essential to (and is a mark of success for) a futures contract. As a rule, the more participants on a futures exchange, the easier it is to buy and sell contracts. This once again highlights the importance of having large numbers of handlers in a particular commodity participate in the futures trade.

In trading parlance, an individual who does not hold stocks is said to be *short the commodity* and establishes a *long futures position* when he agrees to accept delivery of product. A person who holds stocks is *long the commodity* and, upon entering into a contract whereby he agrees to deliver product, is said to have established a *short futures position* in that commodity. Hence, for each contract, there are always corresponding long and short positions.

Most futures contracts can be settled by delivery of the underlying commodity. It is, in fact, not an actual physical delivery of the material, but rather a transfer in title to the contracted quantity of that commodity in a storage facility. The New York Mercantile Exchange's No. 2 heating-oil contract for New York Harbor delivery is an exception, in that it requires that the buyer physically move his product from the tank farm in which it has been stored.

To protect buyer and seller, provisions must be made in the event that the material delivered is not of the standard grade specified in the futures contract. Two basic settlement practices allow for this adjustment. Under the *commercial grade system,* the grade stated in the contract is deliverable at the contract price, while superior grades are deliverable at a premium and inferior grades at a discount. In these cases, the premiums and discounts are negotiated at the time of delivery. Under the *fixed delivery system,* the contract itself stipulates the specific prices that will govern settlement in the event that a nonstandard grade is delivered.

These two pricing systems contribute greatly to the transferability of the contracts by allowing the parties to deal in grades other than the standard ones, while still allowing for an equitable settlement. Both buyer and seller are protected. Within limits, the purchaser need not accept inferior material for the standard-grade price, and the seller will not be required to provide superior grade materials for less than their fair value. Also, these pricing mechanisms prevent a temporary shortage of the standard grade of a commodity from interfering with orderly trade. This is important to maintaining a continuous flow in trading.

Of equal importance, these pricing systems reduce the chance that an individual can *corner* the market in a commodity, by accumulating title to so large an amount of material that he can force others to buy from him in order to fulfill their contractual obligations. Nevertheless, attempts at corners continue to be an occasional traumatic event for various commodities. Veteran metal traders can offer many instructive tales on this subject, most notably in tin, copper, and silver trading.

Trading Futures Contracts

Trading takes place on the floor of the commodity exchange. It is done by the floor traders of the exchange and not by the ultimate parties of a contract. Different exchanges trade different commodities and each has different numbers of floor traders. All members of these exchanges serve the same purpose. They trade futures contracts for their own accounts and on behalf of their clients. Someone wanting to enter a commodity contract notifies his commodity broker, who relays the order through the operations facility of the brokerage firm to a floor member. He in turn buys the contract from another floor trader. This contract is then credited by the trader to the account of the brokerage house, which in turn credits the account of their customer.

The transactions between floor traders are executed by *open outcry.* In this system, the final price of a contract is reached by a verbal exchange of bids and offers among the traders. This classic (and noisy) feature of the commodities exchanges is often cited as the best example of the marketplace in action.

The price-forming service is another major function of commodity-futures exchanges. Because of the continuous participation in futures trading of well-informed commodities handlers, the floor prices are accepted as accurately representing fair market value. The prices arrived at on the futures exchanges are widely used by industry in setting contract and acceptance prices. In futures market terminology, the price of a commodity at any moment is the price of the most actively traded forward position. This price also serves to establish most non-futures prices.

The term *non-futures,* while not used in commodities trading parlance, is used here to refer to fixed merchandising contracts for deferred delivery (forward contracts) and to *spot* or *cash* transactions.

The term non-futures can clarify our thinking and avoid some misconceptions, such as the following three common misunderstandings.

1. The term *futures,* as contrasted with *physicals* or *actuals,* is sometimes thought to mean that futures contracts are mere pieces of paper, which distort the market by representing supplies of oil or other commodities that do not physically or actually exist. This is not so.
2. To the uninformed, the term futures as opposed to cash could suggest that a futures-contract trader is somehow trying to avoid paying. Of course, the seller in a futures contract must either deliver the commodity he owns or make financial settlement during the month in which the obligation becomes due. Likewise, the buyer must pay if he receives title to the commodity or needs to offset his purchase to avoid delivery.
3. The term futures does not always imply deferred delivery. During the month in which it matures a futures contract is a contract for present, almost immediate, delivery.

Because futures contracts are used mainly as financial instruments to establish a position in the market and dampen the effect of price changes, futures trading is less relevant for commodities with a history of relative price stability. The days of price stability for oil are now over. In the absence of sizeable price swings, there is little purpose in not making a forward merchandising contract. Not only is futures trading desirable for a commodity with price swings, such as oil, but the very existence of a futures market contributes to reducing price volatility by providing for speculative trading.

The Commodities Clearinghouse

Basically, futures contracts are entered into unilaterally. That is, the buyer does not know the seller, and vice versa. The contracts are constantly being offset and their ownership transferred, so it is impractical and unnecessary to match ultimate sellers to ultimate buyers. The potential problem of determining the other side to a transaction is remedied by the use of a central clearinghouse for novation—the process by which all the trades executed by the floor traders are netted and new obligations are legally substituted for old ones. Each exchange, with the exception of the London Metal Exchange, has a clearinghouse for novation. This is the practice on the oil-future exchanges.

The floor trader, of course, knows the other party to the transaction and negotiates price with that party. Traders can, however, offset any transaction—that is, transfer the obligation to buy or sell to another party—at their sole discretion and without consideration of the party involved in the original transaction. In this sense, even direct trade between floor traders can be seen as unilateral.

To execute novation, the clearinghouse interposes itself between the buyer and seller in each transaction by assuming the obligations of the other side of each purchase and of each sale. Thus, when a buyer purchases a contract to take delivery of a commodity lot, he is contracting to buy from the clearinghouse. When the contract is settled, either title or money is received from the clearinghouse, which in turn receives title or cash from whatever party is at that time required to make delivery of that commodity under the same contract. The clearing facility's guarantee that it will fulfill all obligations protects each party against the danger of default by the other.

While there is a corresponding spot or cash market in every commodity for which there is futures trading, futures trading is not suitable for every commodity. Futures markets are most useful for commodities that experience price volatility. This fluctuation can be caused by many factors. Wheat, for example, is a commodity for which futures trading came about as a result of the impact of crop seasons. Millers and bakers relying on stored wheat would face higher prices because of limited supply during winter months. Farmers would suffer from depressed prices during harvest season when supplies are plentiful.

Price volatility in the international trade of oil was a major factor in the growth of oil futures. Aside from the effect of the Suez Canal closings in 1956 and 1967, world prices of refined products move up and down with the seasons, but in a limited range. Large price rises and uncertainties arising from government policies prompted the initiation of futures trading in petroleum products, beginning with the trading of gas-oil (No. 2 heating oil) contracts in 1978 on the New York Mercantile Exchange.

The clearinghouse backs this guarantee with reserves accumulated from the deposits that traders are required to pay to assume and to maintain their positions in futures contracts. First, an initial deposit is paid upon establishment of a futures position. In addition to this, on each subsequent day, the contract holder may have to pay a margin deposit to maintain his position if prices change. The margin deposit on a contract equals the difference between its value on the day when an individual assumed the position and its value at the end of each trading day thereafter.

Let us use gold as an example. If one took a long position to buy one hundred ounces of gold at $490 per ounce, an immediate payment would be demanded; this initial deposit might be $2,500. Should the value of the contract fall to $480 per ounce on the following day, there would be a deposit of an additional $10 per ounce, or $1,000 to compensate for the diminished value of the position. If the price of the contract rose on the next day to $505 per ounce, the account would be credited $15 per ounce, or $1,500. This amount which represents equity in excess of that held on the day the initial position was taken, could be withdrawn from the account.

By means of the margin system, constant equity is maintained in an account. When the clearinghouse assumes the sell side of a transaction, it always has equity at its disposal. Should it need to liquidate an account because of the default by a seller on his obligation to deliver, the liquidation value of that account equals the value of its assets on the day a trade was made.

By maintaining the reserve of deposit funds collected for every position assumed in the course of trading, the clearinghouse can compensate buyers financially for the value of a product not delivered if a seller defaults. It also can take delivery and pay a seller in the event of default by a purchaser.

The clearinghouse, in addition to monitoring and regulating trade on the floor of the exchange and enforcing compliance with deposit regulations, serves as the general operations facility for the exchange. It keeps complete records of all trades and price movements, and serves as a central source of this information. As a general business intermediary, moreover, the clearinghouse collects all amounts owed and pays all amounts due, receives and passes title to commodities, and is always able to assume the other side of a transaction so that a buyer or seller will have a party with whom to enter into a contract.

Cash Markets and Futures Markets

Let us briefly compare the commodity-futures markets and cash markets, to see some fundamental differences between them. First, we will examine the purpose of transations in each market.

In the cash market, the purchaser needs the product, and the seller wishes to sell his product and to be paid immediately. The vast majority of trades are settled by delivery. Speculators rarely enter this market because of the relative difficulty of finding another party to sell to when the cash-market price reaches the point at which the speculator wishes to close out. Prior to establishing oil-futures markets, speculators rarely traded oil products on a cash basis.

In the futures market both purchaser and seller seek a position in the market that will enable them to plan for the orderly operation of their businesses.

Very few transactions are settled by actual delivery. Speculators will enter this market because of the ease with which they can offset their contracts at a desirable price.

Next, let us look at the trading method and at how prices are determined. In the cash market, the purchaser and seller directly negotiate a mutually agreeable price. The possibility exists that one party will have to spend a good deal of time and money, contacting many others until a willing partner is located. This can so delay the process that business plans and operations are hampered. Conversely, in the futures market, the parties to a contract each deal through the floor traders of an exchange and are strangers to one another. The price of their contract is determined quickly and smoothly in the competitive exchange of bids and offers.

Activity in the cash market is not well documented. Information concerning the volume of trade or of general price trends is the confidential property of the parties to the relevant transactions. In the futures market, on the other hand, price and volume statistics are made publicly by the commodity-futures exchanges and participating firms. This publicity is important to the exchange, as it attracts turnover. Witness the publication of International Petroleum Exchange trading data each day in the *Financial Times*, or the publication of data from the New York Mercantile Exchange in the *Wall Street Journal.*

Differences in access to the market also exist; in the cash market a party desiring to enter into a cash contract may not be well informed about other potential parties to a contract. This lack of knowledge translates into a significant loss of bargaining power. This problem does not arise in the futures market because everyone has equal access to the entire market at any time and can be assured of obtaining a fair and competitive price.

What about transferability of title and credit risks? While the obligations in a cash contract may be legally transferable, it is not likely that an original party will quickly find a substitute if he is unable to fulfill his obligation. Furthermore, the other side might have something to say about an unexpected substitute buyer or seller whose reliability and credit rating may be in question. Not all contracts permit transfer or assignment of obligations.

These issues do not arise in futures markets. Positions in commodity futures are easily established and contracts are readily transferable by novation. Because the clearinghouse is always the other party to an individual's transaction, the danger of default is avoided, for all practical purposes. However, in the case of default in a cash market, an injured party often must resort to costly and lengthy litigation. Because the clearinghouse acts as arbitrator and as guarantor in all disputes, this possible problem does not arise in a futures-trading situation.

Commodity Handlers

The role of speculators in futures markets is straightforward. These individuals, based on their own projections of price changes, trade futures contracts to profit from expected price moves. Their business otherwise is not related to the speculative commodity. However, in light of the comparison of futures and cash transactions, it may help to consider why someone whose business is linked to a commodity would trade futures contracts. This is especially important to prospects for widening trade in oil futures, because the viability of trade in oil-futures contracts will depend upon the amount of activity generated by oil companies and state oil agencies, as well as brokers. The assurance of a continuous market for a futures contract, created by the activities of many parties, attracts speculators to the market. The infusion of capital from speculation provides added liquidity and continuity to the market.

As for other commodities, there are basically two reasons for oil firms to trade in oil-futures contracts. The first is to establish a temporary substitute for an eventual merchandising contract. The second is to establish a substitute position instead of resorting to the spot market at that future date when the product is to be actually bought and sold.

There are three major justifications for taking a temporary position in the futures market, rather than completing a contract for deferred delivery. The first is that, for some businesses, it is extremely helpful if a purchase of raw material and a corresponding sale of finished product can be made simultaneously. It can greatly aid a mill owner, for example, if he knows the price he will receive for flour at the time he contracts for the purchase of wheat. The process helps set profit margins. It is not, however, the case in the petroleum industry. More than half of world crude-oil trade is in oil from the Organization of Petroleum Exporting Countries (OPEC), and the pricing and profit-margin mechanisms are determined by OPEC collective decisions.

A second reason for futures trading arises when a party willing to enter into a merchandising contract cannot be located at as high a price as could be gotten from a speculator on the futures market. In this instance, a position in a futures contract simply results in a better price.

The third situation requiring the use of a futures contract occurs when efforts to make a merchandising contract at any price are thwarted at a given moment. In this case, the seller is at least assured of a contract on the futures exchange. This assurance is provided by the clearinghouse, and is made economically feasible by the presence of speculators who are willing to make a deal to profit from an anticipated price change.

Thus, a temporary position in futures contracts can reduce or eliminate exposure to loss from adverse price changes and can lock in a profit on corresponding purchase and sale transactions by fixing the spread between the buying and selling price. The mechanics to reach goals with futures contracts are explained in chapter 3.

To summarize briefly, commodity-futures trading makes its most significant contribution to the economy by providing a competitive forum to establish both present and future prices and by furnishing a price-stablizing financial mechanism—the futures contract—to assist in smooth and orderly business operations.

The world oil industry has been able to function smoothly for over a century without futures trading. Control of the logistics of crude oil and finished-products movements has been traditionally with the large private companies, international majors, and leading independents. Now, state companies from OPEC countries and elsewhere have assumed a good part of the responsibility and market power to set curde-oil volume and price levels. Perhaps world market conditions in the oil industry have now changed sufficiently to make a futures market viable. It can only become so if the large operators—majors and state-owned companies—choose to use this type of commodities exchange. If they do not, it may wither away or at best remain a sideshow to the main events of the international petroleum scene.

2

Price Relationships on Futures Markets

Forward Market

During periods of *normal* supply and demand conditions—however that word is defined—futures contracts for delivery in forward months (*deferreds* or *distants*) usually trade at a premium over the cash-market price and over the price of futures contracts for months closer to the present *(nearbys)*. This situation entails a carrying charge, which is often described by professionals by the term *contango*. Included in this carrying charge are the fees which must be paid for storage and insurance, interest expense, and other incidental costs. In the oil trade, product loss due to evaporation is an important consideration in storage. Volatility and flammability render petroleum products expensive to store.

There is a theoretical maximum amount by which the price of a futures contract for a specific delivery month can exceed the price of a futures contract for delivery in any preceeding month. This ceiling carrying charge exists because if the contango was greater than the total of all carrying costs, it would pay to take physical delivery and to arrange for storage. Simply stated, if the contango is more than the carrying costs, it would be cheaper to purchase product for immediate delivery and hold it until needed. Or the purchaser could store the commodity confident of making a profit on the contango by selling futures contracts.

Backwardation

The other side of the contango coin is *backwardation* or the state of affairs when the spot price of a commodity, and the prices of nearbys, are at a premium relative to the prices of contracts for deferred delivery. Backwardation refers also to the actual price difference between contracts in a backwarded market.

Backwardation—or an *inverse carrying charge* market—is an indication of a present shortage of available supply of a commodity. An expected return to normal supply conditions can permit the prices of distants to be lower than current prices. The shortage in supply can be caused by any of several factors, including physical damage to producing facilities, strikes, the imposition of governmental restrictions on exports or imports, a major supplying country's revaluation of its currency, or heavy seasonal restocking demand by users. The oil industry is prone to short-run supply crunches but tends to operate with surplus producing capacity in the long run. Witness the loss of Iranian and Iraqi oil in the wake of their continuing border war and the concurrent glut caused by increased Saudi production and decreased western consumption.

Backwardation also comes from market manipulation by financially influential parties. Control over a sufficiently large amount of available nearby supply permits a *squeeze* on the market, forcing others to bid up the price as they compete with one another for the limited supplies still available. The ultimate act of cornering a market is, of course, in direct conflict with the economic purpose of futures markets and is a flagrant breach of the regulations of futures trading. Most markets maintain sweeping powers to combat the emergence of a corner, including the right to forbid trading by a party whose trading activities are seen to endanger the free-market operations of the exchange. The scale and geographic spread of the world oil trade make it very unlikely that any syndicate can ever amass control over enough of the supply of a product to actually corner the market. That is not to say that a major supplier such as Saudi Arabia cannot be extremely influential in determining short-term prices.

Inasmuch as, for example, the price in July of a futures contract for delivery in November equals the July price plus storage for five months, a backwarded market seems to indicate that there is a *negative price of storage*. This seeming contradiction in terms is reconciled by two related factors. First, a holder of stocks of a commodity usually has an operating income to compensate for what might be considered the opportunity lost by continuing to hold stocks for which he otherwise might be able to receive the current premium price. Thus, what for the buyer is a negative price of storage is for the holder a negative return on storage, representing the profit which a holder could have had by selling inventories. Second, any such unrealized loss is often compensated for by the *convenience yield*—the benefit which accrues by maintaining necessary inventories to run his business operations. The most important feature of an inverse carrying charge market, however, is its effect on the availability of supplies. By providing a premium price to those who bring stocks to the marketplace during a period of backwardation, the negative price of storage brings about the better allocation of a commodity by inducing holders to sell nearby on the market those stocks which exceed the quantity needed to continue business.

Note that contangos or backwardations are not indicative of any basic market trend for a commodity. They are temporary conditions based on immediate supply and demand relationships and are not self-perpetuating. The fact that the market for a certain contract, or commodity, is backwarded on one day does not necessarily imply that it will be so on the next day. The trend of any particular commodity-futures contract is determined only in relation to its historical behavior and is derived by comparing today's price of a contract for delivery six months in the future with one for six months delivery as of yesterday, last week, or the previous year.

Intercontract Price Relationships

The prices of contracts for different delivery months generally move in the same direction, and changes in the price of one contract will usually be matched by a similar percentage change in the price of another. This basic linkage of price changes, and the resulting stability of price spread between different maturity months, is preserved by the equilibrating forces exerted by arbitrage. The use of futures contracts for delivery of supply also helps maintain the relationship between prices for different delivery months.

Arbitrage, generally speaking, is a trading operation that depends for profit on the difference existing at any particular time in the prices of the same item on different markets. In futures trading, different delivery months are, in effect, different markets, and each has its own supply and demand relationships. Thus, if in July a contract to buy gas oil for December delivery can be entered into at approximately $350 per tonne when the price of gas oil on a September futures contract is about $335 per tonne and the carrying charge for four months is $6 per tonne, an individual could contract to buy on a September contract at, per-haps, $336 per tonne and simultaneously go short for December delivery at $349 per tonne. (A seller will always receive a price slightly lower than that which the buyer in the same transaction will have to pay; the difference be-tween the two is paid to the floor trader.) By virtue of these complementary commitments, the arbitrageur has made a transaction profit of $13 per tonne. To arrive at the effective net gain realized from these trades, the cost of storage from September through December is deducted from the $13 per tonne figure.

Such an opportunity for arbitrage will increase demand for the September futures contract—raising its price—and increase the supply of the commodity made available for delivery by the December futures contract—lowering its price—until the difference in price between the two more closely approximates the actual storage cost for the four-month period. In this manner, the market is self-regulating with respect to pricing.

A significant difference in price between futures contracts of different maturities can lead to the use of futures for delivery, as well. Using the same figures as in the previous example, an individual who knows in July that he will need gas oil in December can assume a long position in the September con-tract, take delivery of the underlying commodity in September, and store it on his own until December. Likewise, holders of gas oil who wish to sell some of their stock can try to take advantage of the relatively high-priced December con-tract. The increased demand for September contracts on the part of gas oil buyers and the decreased amount of supply offered through that contract will raise its price. The increased supply of December contracts by heating oil sellers, and the decreased demand for the December contract, will reduce its price. Thus the difference in price between the September and December contracts will approach the actual cost of storage for the four-month period.

If the price of a deferred future is less than the sum of the price of a nearby plus the cost of storage through the maturity month of the deferred, an opposite set of transactions can be effected. In the last example, had the price of gas oil on the December contract been $239 per tonne instead of $350, the buyer could go long on the December contract because he could save $2 per tonne by not storing the gas oil himself. The seller could go short on the September contract to save the $2 per tonne that he would lose if he made his own storage arrangements until making delivery in December. Demand by buyers increases and seller-sponsored supply decreases for the December contract, pushing its price up, while the September price falls because of decreased demand and greater supply. These opposite price movements will lessen significantly when the proper relationship between the price of the distant and that of the nearby is reestablished.

The Bases

The *bases* are the relationships between the cash price and the futures-market price. There are three such relationships. The first is the *maturity basis,* the difference between the price of a futures contract trading in its maturity month and the current cash price. The second is the *basis* or the difference between the current spot-market price and the price of a futures contract prior to its maturity month. Finally, there is the *forward basis* or the difference between the price of a futures contract trading in a month prior to its maturity and the cash price for forward delivery in that same month.

Each of the three bases are maintained, as is the relationship between the prices of futures contracts for various delivery months, by the equilibrating forces of arbitrage and settlement by delivery.

Maturity Basis

Under normal market conditions, the maturity basis increases progressively for successive delivery months, reflecting the additional carrying costs incurred in the storage of supplies. As its delivery month nears, the price of a futures contract and the spot price of the underlying commodity will tend to approach one another.

Were the cash price to be significantly higher than the futures-contract price for that same month, the demand on the part of buyers for the spot-market product would decline as the demand for the lower-priced futures contract increased. Inventory holders would try to sell on the cash market rather than commit to make delivery on the lower-priced futures market. This.

increase of available supply, along with decreased demand, on the cash market would cause the cash-market price to decline; the corresponding decrease of supply and increase of demand on the futures market would cause futures prices to rise. At the same time, arbitrageurs would contract to take delivery on the futures market to take advantage of the profit to be made by simultaneously selling on the higher-priced cash market. Eventually, as a result of these operations, the basis would narrow to the point at which such transactions would no longer permit any profit.

In the event that the price of a futures contract, in its delivery month, were to exceed to any appreciable degree the prevailing cash price, similar but opposite forces would diminish the basis. Buyers would try to purchase on the lower-priced cash market at the same time that sellers would try to sell their stocks on the higher-priced futures market. The higher demand and lower supply on the cash market would elevate its price, as the futures price is driven down by falling demand and increasing supply.

Arbitrageurs, however, contribute to the increased demand on the cash market, as well as to the increased supply being made available through the futures market. Thus, as before, the cash and the futures price will converge until equilibrium is attained.

In its maturity month, a futures contract will most likely trade at a small discount to the spot price. This discount reflects the slight undesirability of a maturing contract caused by the possible inconvenience and expense to the buyer of entering into a contract for which he does not know the exact date, or place, of delivery. In many cases, for example, a seller can make immediate delivery of a commodity under a current contract, but the buyer may not wish to take delivery anywhere or any time, a prerogative the buyer enjoys with a futures contract.

The Basis

Usually, the *basis* will approximate the cost of storage between the present month and the delivery month of the contract. Were the price in July for a November futures contract for heating oil to exceed the July cash price by more than the cost of storage from July through November, buyers would rather purchase on the cash market and pay for storage themselves. Arbitrageurs would enter the market to buy on the cash market and, at the same time, to contract to sell the commodity on the higher priced November futures market. The resulting increase in demand and decrease of supply on the cash market would increase that price, and falling demand for the futures contract would bring its price down, until the basis is restored.

Were the November futures contracts selling at a discount relative to the spot-market price plus storage for five months, the opposite trading pattern would emerge. Buyers, would postpone taking delivery of the commodity and forgo an immediate cash market purchase to take advantage of the lower price (after storage is considered) of the material through the November futures contract. Suppliers would sell into the spot market to avoid the loss they would incur by storing the material at their own expense for five months and then selling. Such transactions will be arrested by natural market forces when the basis is returned to the point at which profitable trades can no longer be made.

Forward Basis

The integrity of the forward basis is maintained in a similar manner. If in July a forward contract for No. 2 oil can be arranged for November delivery at a total price, including storage costs, of $305 per tonne, arbitrage transactions and normal user trading will reduce this $10 per tonne difference. Similarly, were a forward contract to cost $325 per tonne, buyers would increase supply demand on the futures market, and sellers would increase supply on the spot market, shrinking the basis to the point where the transaction costs of trades would offset any profit to be derived from any price differential between the two markets.

3 Trading Commodity-Futures Contracts

Basic Trading Strategies

Now that we have touched upon the mechanics of futures trading, we will examine how futures markets are used in practice. We will begin by reviewing the three primary types of trade: hedging, speculation, and arbitrage. While the differences between these trading forms cannot be seen on the floor of an exchange, they matter a great deal to the persons on whose behalf those trades are carried out.

Simply put, hedging is a trade involving simultaneous positions in the futures market and the cash market. Hedges serve as temporary substitutes for eventual merchandising agreements. There are various reasons why hedges are undertaken, and we will discuss these shortly. Hedging accounts for the majority of transactions on a futures exchange, and the oil futures exchanges are no exception.

Speculation, which contributes to the liquidity necessary for the effective conduct of a futures exchange, is trading in anticipation of price movements. It is a trading operation that seeks to profit from being either long or short, depending on how price movements are expected to go.

Arbitrage seeks to profit from the differences that exist, at any time, between the price at which an item can be purchased and the price at which that same item can be sold. If a person can buy something on one market and simultaneously or immediately thereafter sell that same item on another market at a higher price, arbitrage transactions become practicable. Arbitrage technically is not speculation because there is no reliance on expectations of price changes. Rather, the transactions are at currently existing prices. Crude-oil traders are old hands at the arbitrage game, and it is not unknown for one of them to buy from and sell back to the same multinational corporate giant on the same afternoon.

Hedging

The biggest segment of commodity-futures trading is traditionally described as *hedging*. Hedging involves taking a position in the futures market that is equal in quantity but opposite in obligation to the position held in the cash market. It is

19

a trading strategy which minimizes loss in the event of unexpected adverse price changes in the cash market.

While it is true that hedging, by virtue of its mechanics, diminishes the effect of absolute price changes, it is not right to say hedging is only used to reduce risks. Risk reduction can be only incidental to a hedge. The common use of the term *hedging* to refer to an automatic reliance on the futures market solely to reduce risk attributes to commodity handlers a passivity that is atypical of them. Hedging is not always a reflex operation undertaken to decrease the risk of loss. It is also a sophisticated trading method, often based on specific expectations of future price relationships. Successful hedging locks in the price at which the product will eventually be bought or sold, by establishing at a prior date a position that serves as a temporary substitute for an eventual merchandising contract.

A hedge has two *legs*—the *cash leg* and the *futures leg*. Each leg consists of two transactions—the assumption of a long position and the assumption of a short position. The term *long hedge* denotes a group of at least four transactions in which the initial position in the futures market is a contract to accept delivery of product; a *short hedge* is one in which the trader's initial futures position is a contract to make delivery.

A short hedge is used by a seller who wishes to fix, to a high degree, the price at which he ultimately will sell. Short hedges also establish the value of inventory. A long hedge, on the other hand, is used by a buyer who wishes to fix the price that he will ultimately pay.

At the closing of a hedge, the price that matters most to the hedger will be the price at which the initial cash-market position was established. This cash price governs the economics of the ultimate physical transaction, as far as the hedger is concerned. Changes in the price of a futures contract over time and not the absolute prices themselves are important for a successful hedge. The futures leg of a hedge does not directly govern the ultimate delivery price but serves as a financial mechanism that diminishes the effect of price changes in the cash market.

Short Hedge. For example, if in January a distributor who is long on gas oil in the cash market projects that the spot price of gas oil will decline by May, he can assure himself of receiving close to the current cash price, at some later date, by contracting in January to sell on the futures market. Thus, if the spot price declines as he had forecasted, he will make a profit in May when he covers his original short position in the futures market, because he will be able to establish an offsetting long-futures position to purchase product at a price lower than that at which he agreed to sell. Because cash-market and futures-market prices generally move together, the gain made on the futures market should closely approximate the corresponding loss incurred on the cash market. The series of events making up this type of short-hedge operation is illustrated in the following example.

1. In January, distributor D agrees to provide one thousand tonnes of gas oil to customer C in May at the May spot price. The current market value of his gas oil inventory—that is, the current prevailing spot-market price—is $280 per tonne, accordingly, D is long one thousand tonnes at $280 per tonne.
2. To determine in January, to a reasonable degree, the price that he will realize from the May sale to C of gas oil, the distributor wishes to initiate a short hedge by commiting in the futures market to make delivery in May of one thousand tonnes of product. He does this by going short on ten contracts, each for one hundred tonnes, at $296 per tonne.
3. In May, the prevailing spot-market price is $260 per tonne, at which price D sells gas oil to C. As he was long gas oil in January at $280 per tonne, D has incurred an unrealized loss of $20 per tonne on his cash-market position (not taking into account his cost of storage from January through May).
4. D now completes his hedge by establishing a long futures position on ten contracts, thus offsetting his obligation, which has not matured, to deliver gas oil. The price at which his long position is established is $259 per tonne; he has thus scored a gain of $37 per tonne on the futures leg of his hedge.

The overall result of the distributor's short hedge is represented in table 3-1.

The distributor has sold product for $260 per tonne, but also has a hedging profit of $17 per tonne, raising revenues to $277 per tonne. Because the price has declined, however, D has an unrealized loss from storing gas oil between January through May. If storage costs were $9 per tonne, the distributor's net revenues would be reduced to $268 per tonne. However, the unrealized loss on storage would not affect the distributor, as normal business decisions take storage costs into account. The important thing is how the hedging sequence improved his situation: with no hedge, D would have received only $260 per tonne, from which amount he would still have to deduct storage costs. By hedging, he grossed $277 per tonne, much closer to the January price of $280 than to the May price of $260 per tonne.

Table 3-1
Short Hedge

	January	May	Transaction Outcome
Cash market	Long at $280/tonne	Short at $260/tonne	Loss of $20/tonne
Futures market	Short at $296/tonne	Long at $259/tonne	Gain of $37/tonne
Outcome of hedge			Net gain of $17/ton

In a rising market, the result of the loss incurred on the futures leg of a short hedge will be to reduce the profit realized on the cash-market leg. Should the hedger project, however, that the rising price trend will continue, he can offset his original futures position before its maturity to maximize the profit on his spot-market transactions.

A short hedge in a rising market is represented in table 3-2.

Had the distributor correctly decided to lift his hedge in February, however, based upon an expectation that prices would continue to rise, his profit could have been greater, as table 3-3 shows.

Maintaining a short hedge in a continually rising market is symptomatic of pure insurance, or risk reduction, hedging. This sort of hedge will reduce one's profit, and it is unlikely that this position would be maintained indefinitely by professionals. A hedge, once removed, can be reestablished quickly if prices start to change direction. Sellers would rather make a profit than have price protection insurance when this insurance only protects them from greater profit!

Table 3-2
Short Hedge in Rising Market

	January	May	Transaction Outcome
Cash market	Long at $280/tonne	Short at $300/tonne	Gain of $20/tonne
Futures market	Short at $290/tonne	Long at $299/tonne	Loss of $9/tonne
Outcome of hedge			Net gain of $11/tonne

Table 3-3
Short Hedge in Continuously Rising Market

	January	February	May	Transaction Outcome
Cash market	Long at $280/tonne		Short at $300/tonne	Gain of $20/tonne
Futures market	Short at $290/tonne	Long at $291.50/tonne		Loss of $1.50/tonne
Outcome of hedge				Net gain of $18.50/ tonne

There are instances when even a well-informed party would maintain a short hedge in a rising market. One important case is when inventory has been used to obtain a bank loan. While stocks normally cannot be borrowed against if there is any uncertainty of their market value over the long term, hedged stocks can be used for collateral because their value is protected. Of course, the bank should establish loan terms so the hedge could be lifted and subsequently reassumed where commercial wisdom would so dictate.

Such short hedging, however, does not typify short-term actions by persons familiar with the oil products trade. Because hedging can be a profitable venture in and of itself, the profit motive—and not price insurance—generally motivates the hedging transactions.

Long Hedge. The following series of events illustrate a buyer's long hedge.

1. In January customer C enters into a contract with distributor D to purchase one thousand tonnes of gas oil at the May market price. The spot price in January is $280 per tonne; C believes that this price will rise. To protect himself against any price increase, he hedges his future purchase by establishing a long futures position in ten gas oil contracts, each for one hundred tonnes, for May delivery. He buys these contracts at $288 per tonne.
2. In early May C purchases one thousand tonnes of gas oil from D at $320 per tonne, the prevailing spot-market price at the time. C closes out by going short ten gas oil futures contracts at $319 per tonne, the price at which these contracts were negotiated on the floor of the exchange, to offset his original long futures position.
3. C has an unrealized loss of $40 per tonne on his cash-market transactions and a profit of $31 per tonne on the futures leg of his hedge. The overall result of this hedge to C is a loss of $9 per tonne.

This hedge is schematically presented in table 3–4.

Because customer C was short product and expected the price of gas oil to rise over the short-term, he established a long position on the futures market. This obligation to accept delivery of one thousand tonnes of gas oil at $288 per tonne is offset (before the contract expires) through novation by a contract to deliver product at $319 per tonne. This $31 per tonne hedging gain reduces the customer's cash-market price of $320 per tonne by $31, to an effective purchase price of $289 per tonne. In actuality he will pay $320 per tonne in cash to the distributor; this figure is not altered by his hedging transactions.

The essential element of a successful hedge is the parallelism of movement between prices in the cash and futures markets. While the actual change in prices on the two markets will usually not be identical, the overall effect of any absolute price change is significantly diminished.

Table 3–4
Long Hedge

	January	May	Transaction Outcome
Cash market	Short at $280/tonne	Long at $320/tonne	Loss of $40/tonne
Futures market	Long at $288/tonne	Short at $319/tonne	Gain of $31/tonne
Outcome of hedge			Net loss of $9/tonne

The effect of establishing a long hedge in a falling market would be similar to maintaining a short hedge through a period of rising prices. It reduces the unrealized gain that could be made on the cash-market leg and incurs a transactions loss on the futures leg. For this reason, such a hedge is generally symptomatic of purely reflex hedging, or of the hedger's belief that a sudden change in the direction of price movement is imminent.

Hedging Types. While hedging transactions always consist of the same components, there can be great latent differences between any two hedging transactions. The difference is one of intent, or why the hedge has been executed.

Though hedging has traditionally been referred to as a risk-reduction mechanism that serves as a type of insurance against adverse price changes, it must be stressed that this is only one of the motives to hedge. Five types of hedging have been noted, and in only one case is the minimization of exposure to risk the primary impetus for the hedge. This does not mean that the risk-reduction element is unimportant to the handler with a different primary motive. Yet price expectation is, in most cases, a strong presence behind the execution of a hedge. The passivity of a reflex hedge is the exception among hedging transactions and not the rule. A detailed look at four strategies for hedging will demonstrate how these types of hedges differ from each other.

Carrying-Charge Hedging. This form of hedging is based on the desire to profit directly from storage operations. Carrying-charge hedging is dependent for profit not on changes in the absolute price levels of a particular commodity, but rather on changes in the basis. An anticipated decrease in the basis will prompt a carrying-charge hedger who is long product to initiate a short hedge; an expected increase will prompt a long hedge to be undertaken.

In table 3–5, the absolute price of the commodity traded has decreased. The trader made a profit because the basis has decreased from $4/lot to $2/lot. Had the commodity price risen, the short hedger could still have a gain, as long as the basis had narrowed, as shown in table 3–6.

Table 3-5
Short Hedge, with Basis Decrease and Commodity Price Decrease

	January	May	Transaction Outcome
Cash market	Long at $10/lot	Price decrease to $8/lot	Unrealized loss of $2/lot
Futures market	Short at $14/lot for March delivery	Price decrease to $10/lot	Gain of $4/lot
Outcome of hedge			Net gain of $2/lot

Table 3-6
Short Hedge, with Basis Decrease and Commodity Price Increase

	January	May	Transaction Outcome
Cash market	Long at $10/lot	Short at $18/lot	Gain of $8/lot
Futures market	Short at $14/lot	Long at $20/lot	Loss of $6/lot
Outcome of hedge			Net gain of $2/lot

In general, when producers and those who use oil products as raw materials decide to store for profit, they prefer to seek the profit by anticipating changes in the absolute price level of a commodity. Distributors, on the other hand, are more likely to seek profit by anticipating changes in price relations.

Whereas the traditional definition of hedging attributes the hedging decision to price expectations, carrying-charge hedging hinges on the decision of whether or not to store product in anticipation of the resultant hedging transaction's ability to bring profit.

Selective Hedging. Selective hedging is a practice based upon expectations of absolute price levels. The aim is not to avoid risk, but to minimize or altogether avoid any loss that could be incurred by holding stocks during a declining market. Through such hedging traders actively participate in the price-forming process by pressuring the marketplace according to their expectations of absolute price levels. Selective hedging is usually engaged in by companies maintaining large inventories, such as large oil-refining companies.

Anticipatory Hedging. An anticipatory hedge tries to take advantage of the current price of a commodity and increase the smoothness of business operations. The major difference between anticipatory and other types of hedging is that it comes before, rather than simultaneous with, an equivalent inventory or a formal merchandising agreement. Thus, as its name implies, the time element is essential to an anticipatory hedge which serves as a temporary substitute for an eventual merchandising contract. Processors can go long in futures to hedge against their raw material requirements, and sellers can go short as a substitute for a forward sale of specific goods that are not yet made. Most long hedging is anticipatory hedging of yet-to-be consummated forward contracts.

Operational Hedging. Operational hedging, used primarily by refiners and marketers, involves opening and closing hedges in quick succession to facilitate the orderly operation of business. This hedging strategy is pursued only when there is sufficient price volatility and must be accomplished fast, with time measured in days or even hours. Because of the speed with which such transactions are undertaken, there has to be a high correlation between the spot price and the future price of the hedged commodity.

Basis Trading. Because the change in the futures price of a commodity is unlikely to exactly equal the change in the spot price, the precise outcome of a regular hedging transaction cannot be known in advance. As a consequence, and also as a logical extension to futures trading of the non-futures mechanism of *cost plus* forward contracts, the practice of *basis trading* developed.

Basis trading is a hedging system in which the basis—the relationship between cash and futures prices that actually governs the outcome of a hedge—is agreed to by both parties to a transaction, although the absolute price at which that transaction will occur is not set. The steps in a simple basis trade are these.

1. In September distributor *D* is long gas oil when the cash-market price is $350 per tonne. *D*'s favorite customer (*C*) wants product, but wishes to buy in December because he believes the price is going to decline.
2. As the December futures contracts are currently selling at $355 per tonne—a basis of 5—and as *D* requires a narrowing in the basis to profit from a short hedge, *D* agrees to sell product to *C* in December, at an undetermined absolute price, so long as the eventual price is less than $5 per tonne under the futures price in December. For this example, we shall assume that the distributor wants to establish a basis of 1, and thus contracts to sell to *C* at *1 under December;* that is, at $1 per tonne under the December futures price. Product delivery is *on buyer's call,* that is, at any point before the expiration of the contract at which the customer wishes to accept the gas oil.

3. December comes. *C* was right, and the spot price has fallen significantly. He now decides to purchase product. *C* contacts *D's* broker and directs him to buy December futures contracts for the distributor's account. If the purchase is executed at $251 per tonne, then, in accordance with the *1 under December* provision of the agreement reached between the two parties in September, the customer will pay the distributor $250 per tonne for the gas oil he has committed to purchase.

These steps are schematically represented in figure 3-1.

Thus, through short hedging, distributor *D* has protected himself against a decline in the price of gas oil and, through basis trading, has fixed in advance the profit he will make on the eventual physical sale of product to *C*. The customer has also benefitted: he has locked-in a source of supply in September and will pay the lower December price when he actually accepts delivery of gas oil later in the year.

Speculation

Speculation is a trading method based upon specific expectations of future price changes. It derives profit, in the case of an initial long position, from the appreciation in value of a commodity, and in the case of an initial short position, from the commodity's depreciation in value. It derives losses when the opposite price movements happen, which is why everyone is not a speculator. Successful speculators may skip over these next few paragraphs; less than successful speculators may wish to do so also, because experience is the best teacher. It is a pity, however, that we have to keep taking all those tests!

The simplest form of speculation is a one-leg trade. If you expect the price of a commodity to increase (decrease), go long (short) with the intention of ultimately offsetting this original transaction with an opposing short (long) trade, thus taking a gain by having sold product at a price higher than that at which it is bought.

A speculative trading method with a sequence resembling hedging is the straddle or spread. A spread is a two-legged trading sequence whereby the trader initiates a long and a short futures position simultaneously, but in contracts for different delivery months. In this way the eventual gain on the initial long position, if the price of the contract is expected to increase, will be reduced by the corresponding loss incurred on the initial short position. On the other hand, should the market decline when the speculator had forecasted a rise, the loss he incurs on his initial long position will be reduced by the gain made on his initial short position.

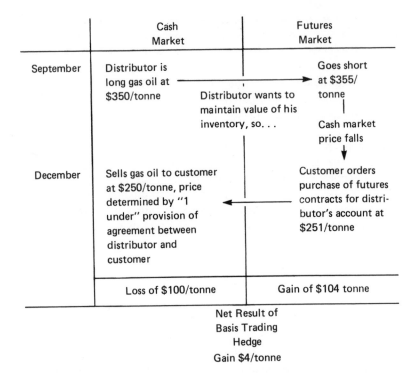

Figure 3-1. Basis Trading Hedge

A straddle is a way to reduce exposure to loss on speculative trading. The reduced profit realized on a straddle as opposed to that possible on a one-legged spread is the price paid to protect against a loss suffered in the event of unfavorable and unexpected market price behavior.

Arbitrage

Arbitrage derives profit from the difference, at any time, between the price at which a commodity can be purchased and the price at which that same commodity can be sold. Arbitrage in commodity-futures contracts consists of the simultaneous establishment of both a long and short position in futures contracts.

There are two basic kinds of arbitrage: *intramarket* and *intermarket.* Intramarket arbitrage consists of establishing opposite commitments simultaneously in one market. As an example, you could commit to purchase gas oil at $300 per tonne pursuant to a December delivery contract and at the same time commit to deliver gas oil in January pursuant to a contract for that month at $310 per tonne, if you believed that the $10 per tonne price difference between the two delivery months would be sufficient to allow a gain after the related storage and transaction costs are taken into consideration. In this example the different delivery months take on the aspects of different markets; you would be buying on the December market and selling on the January market.

Intermarket arbitrage involves buying on one market, or on one exchange, and simultaneously selling on another. Intermarket arbitrage in commodity-futures contracts is thus limited to those commodities that trade on more than one exchange. At present, these include such commodities as wheat, gold, and gas oil. Gas oil is traded on the New York Mercantile Exchange (NYMEX) and on the International Petroleum Exchange (IPE), and a proposal to permit its trading on the Chicago Board of Trade (CBT) is currently under review by the U.S. Commodity Futures regulatory agency. A complete listing of commodity-futures exchanges and of the commodities traded on each is included as appendix F.

Because differences in the prices of one item are generally not very large, the percentage return on arbitrage transactions is usually not very high. Arbitrage is best suited to well-capitalized institutions willing to accept a relatively small percentage gain to score a significant dollar gain.

Day Trading by Floor Traders. Day trading by floor traders is, theoretically, a form of intramarket arbitrage. This trading practice, commonly known as *scalping,* refers to matched purchase and sale transactions executed by a floor trader within one day for his own account. By virtue of his situation, the floor trader is generally able with relative ease to assume and then to offset a position at some profit. Such trades can often be executed almost simultaneously. Day trading of this type is a marginal trading practice and depends for profitability on the volume of transactions executed.

In all the types of trades that might be made on an oil-futures market, certain basic relationships must be maintained in order for them to succeed. The market must be able to attract enough speculation for sufficient fluidity. Without the volume of trade generated by speculation, transaction costs would not be low enough to provide incentive for hedgers who must bear the cost of futures transactions in addition to the cost of eventual merchandising contracts. Speculation could not exist, however, without a firm trading base provided by refiners, shippers, distributors, and customers. By definition, speculators hope to make gains by assuming the risk shed by hedgers.

There are three basic reasons why oil-futures trading might fail. First, the amount of potential use by handlers may be too small to provide an effective price-determination forum. Second, the amount of speculation attracted to the market could be too low to provide the level of fluidity required to sustain active trading. Finally, after having attracted all the speculation and merchandising trade it can, the transaction costs may by too high to attract sufficient use by hedgers. It is too early to judge whether the oil futures markets in London, New York, and other U.S. centers can remain viable. Signs of success are there, but more time will be needed for a clear pattern to emerge.

**Part II
International Petroleum:
Traders and Markets**

4 Multinational Oil Firms

The international petroleum industry today is different both from the orderly world trade structure established by the multinational oil companies in the first half of this century and from the diffuse market which emerged in the wake of OPEC in the early 1970s. The evolution of the world oil industry began with an oligopolistic market, with company control over all vital aspects of exploration, production, and marketing. Under a combination of political and economic forces, the industry unraveled into a diverse, decentralized market with a multiplicity of important decision makers and numerous buyers, sellers, brokers, and middlemen. To a large degree, OPEC's petroleum power and the international oil industry rest upon the industrial and marketing framework built by a very few companies.

To understand today's petroleum market—its forces and influences, as well as its patterns and disruptions—it is necessary to trace the origin, development, and structure of the international industry. While the history in chapters 4 and 5 pre-dates the futures trade in petroleum and focuses on the evolution of the crude-oil industry, it provides an important background for an appreciation of the current state of the world oil market. Similarly, the following sections on the Rotterdam market and oil trading address issues salient to the mechanics of the international oil industry and are part of the larger context of the petroleum-futures trade.

The Emergence of Multinational Oil

During its beginning stages in the latter half of the nineteenth century, the oil industry was comprised of many small producers, refiners, and marketers. By the 1880s, however, the industry began to display a pattern of domination by a few large multinational firms that was to characterize it until the 1970s. At the turn of the century, when J.D. Rockefeller's Standard Oil Trust was achieving near-total control in the United States, Royal Dutch was consolidating its interest in the East Indies, Shell was dominating the markets of the Far East, British interests were controlling the Indian market through the Burmah Oil Company, and Russian companies were producing Rumanian oil.

While some large companies began operating in only one sector of the industry—for instance, Standard Oil in refinery operations—several firms recognized the greater profits to be gained from developing large integrated operations.

Companies increasingly began to integrate upstream into crude-oil production and downstream into refining and marketing. Through the advantages of multinational integration, international coordination, and absolute control over operations at all stages of the industry, power in the world petroleum industry became concentrated in the large vertically integrated firms.

The growing emphasis on owning crude oil at its source led many private companies to look toward the vast unexplored areas of the Middle East. In 1901, the first Middle East concession was given to William D'Arcy by the Shah of Persia. Granted for a period of sixty years and extending over some 500,000 square miles, the agreement covered nearly five-sixths of what today is Iran. This concession was taken over in 1909 by the Anglo-Persian Oil Company (later called Anglo-Iranian Oil Company, and now British Petroleum). In this same period, British, German, and other European interests were seeking oil concessions in Mesopotamia (present-day Iraq), which was part of the Ottoman Empire. European competition for the Ottoman concession was especially acute, and the various interests succeeded only in blocking the others in their attempts to gain access to the oil. Finally, in October 1912, convinced that access to Mesopotamian oil could be gained only by cooperation, the competing interests were reconciled and the Turkish Petroleum Company (TPC) was established (renamed the Iraq Petroleum Company [IPC] in 1929). Ownership of the company was divided, with 50 percent held by the National Bank of Turkey (of which 5 percent was held for C.S. Gulbenkian, architect of the TPC); 25 percent by the Deutsche Bank of Germany; and 25 percent by the Anglo-Saxon Petroleum Company, a subsidiary of Royal Dutch/Shell (Royal Dutch and Shell merged in 1907).

During this period of rivalry for Middle East oil concessions, Great Britain began converting the British Navy from coal to oil-fueled ships. In July 1913, Winston Churchill, then First Lord of the Admiralty, announced the Admiralty's intention to become "the owners, or at any rate the controllers at the source" of their crude supplies.[1] In keeping with their new strategic interest in obtaining and controlling Middle East oil, the British government began actively to support the D'Arcy group and Anglo-Persian in their bid to join the Turkish Petroleum Company, from which they originally had been excluded.

Pressured by the British government, the owners of TPC admitted these new members. In March 1914, the "Foreign Office Agreement" (so-named because the meeting was held in the British Foreign Office) gave a 50 percent interest in the Turkish Petroleum Company to the D'Arcy group, which was acting for Anglo-Persian. The Deutsche Bank and Anglo-Saxon Petroleum Company each received a 25 percent share, from which they equally contributed 2.5 percent toward a 5 percent beneficiary interest for Mr. Gulbenkian. Shortly after the agreement was signed, the British government bought a 51 percent controlling interest in the Anglo-Persian Oil Company, thereby obtaining Persian oil reserves for the government, as well as providing financing for the production of oil by Anglo-Persian.

The outbreak of World War I interrupted the rush to obtain oil concessions. After the war, however, attention was once again focused on the Middle East, as major companies, actively supported by their governments, sought foreign oil to satisfy growing world demand. The postwar dismemberment of the Ottoman Empire focused on the area's rich oil reserves. The 1920 French-British San Remo Agreement allowed the French government to assume the Deutsche Bank's 25 percent stake in TPC, in exchange for allowing the construction of a British pipeline across the French sphere of influence in Syria. If the agreement had been put into effect, U.S. and other companies would have been excluded from the entire area, and the large reserves of the Middle East would have been left solely under British and French control.

Prior to 1920, U.S. companies were not involved in the search for Middle East concessions. Initially concentrating on developing the large reserves in the United States, and blocked from acquiring eastern hemisphere oil by the colonial policies of the European governments and private oil companies, U.S. company oil holdings abroad were negligible at the end of World War I. Fears of a projected oil shortage in the United States, however, and concern over a possible monopoly of foreign reserves by British and Dutch interests, prompted U.S. companies and the U.S. government to look for new sources of crude oil in the Middle East. Not only did the Middle East offer potentially large oil reserves that were closer to major European markets than was U.S. oil, but local rulers also offered access to oil at extremely generous terms. Concessions were usually granted for vast areas—such as the D'Arcy concession in Persia—and in several cases were for entire countries. In addition, concessions were generally granted for lengthy periods, usually sixty to seventy-five years or longer; areas that went unexploited did not have to be relinquished by the companies; host governments did not levy income taxes and received fixed minimal royalty payments; and political and private restrictions on concessions were negligible, as the host governments had no voice in the management or conduct of petroleum operations.

The U.S. government began to pressure the British government to allow U.S. companies access to the areas under British mandate in the Middle East. The United States claimed that an open-door policy should prevail, whereby there would be no monopoly concession, nor would non-British firms be excluded from acquiring concession rights in the area. In 1922, the British government conceded, and negotiations began toward the eventual participation by seven U.S. companies in the Turkish Petroleum Company. The talks dragged on for three years, in which time two of the U.S. companies—Sinclair and Texas Company (later Texaco)—dropped out. In July 1928, an agreement was reached by which five U.S. companies divided a 23.75 percent interest. By 1931, three more U.S. firms withdrew, and the U.S. interest was shared by only Standard Oil Company of New York (Socony, then Socony-Vacuum, now Mobil) and Standard Oil Company of New Jersey (now Exxon). The French government's interests were represented through the 23.75 percent share held by Compagnie Francaise de Pétroles (CFP), a national company established to hold France's interest in TPC. Royal Dutch Shell and Anglo-Persian also each received 23.75 percent, and Mr. Gulbenkian kept his 5 percent.

Dividing the Market: Agreements and Coordination

Once the open door had been achieved, and U.S. companies had gained access to the development of Middle East oil, the door was promptly closed again. Contrary to the U.S. fears of a domestic oil shortage that were prevalent in 1922, by the late 1920s the companies were concerned about a possible glut of oil on world markets. Recognizing the common threat posed to TPC participants by the appearance of a surplus of cheap crude oil, the member companies signed the Red Line agreement in July 1928. Within a red-pencilled area, the signatories agreed to operate only through the TPC and were obligated not to "seek for or obtain or be interested, directly or indirectly, in the production of oil within the defined area or in the purchase of any such oil otherwise than through the Turkish company."[2] This arrangement effectively eliminated competition between the TPC participants in concession-seeking and crude-oil production, purchasing, and refining in an area encompassing most of the former Ottoman Empire, and covering present-day Turkey, Syria, Jordan, Israel, Iraq, and Saudi Arabia. Significantly, it did not include Kuwait or the off-shore islands of Bahrain; nor did it cover Iran, the concession for which was still held by Anglo-Persian. The provisions of the agreement gave TPC a monopoly on concession and production rights, eliminated competition between members of TPC within a large area, and precluded the sharing of the concession with non-members. Through the Red Line agreement, the Turkish Petroleum Company became a multi-firm condominium, and the company was operated not as an independent profit-making concern, but rather as a partnership for the production and sharing of crude oil between its owners.

The Turkish (and later Iraq) Petroleum Company, as the first joint venture in the Middle East, was the archetype for subsequent joint-venture agreements. Joint ventures among the major companies for sharing the ownership and production rights of oil concessions, supplemented by long-term sales contracts and market-sharing agreements, were the instruments for control of the international oil industry. In time, the Seven Sisters—as Shell, Exxon, British Petroleum, Gulf, Standard Oil of California, Mobil, and Texaco came to be jointly known—developed a series of joint-concession arrangements crisscrossing the Middle East in the 1940s and 1950s. Table 4-1 indicates the interrelationships between the eight majors (the Seven Sisters plus CFP) in the Middle East.

The mutual interest in avoiding a world oil glut that produced the Red Line agreement, also led Royal Dutch/Shell, Anglo-Persian, and the Standard Oil of New Jersey, all IPC members, to begin discussions in 1928 toward achieving some form of market control. These three oil companies were then the world's largest, and their collaboration would allow them to control a sizeable share of the world market and to protect their individual interests.

The major impetus behind their meeting was a price war in 1926. World oil production had grown enormously in the 1920s, as Anglo-Persian lifted oil out of Iran, additional fields in Iraq were brought onstream, and new oil from Mexico and Venezuela was entering world markets. By the late 1920s there was a world surplus of oil and a soft market. An attempt by Royal Dutch/Shell to undercut Standard Oil of New York's position in the Far East by selling large quantities of cheap Russian oil led Standard to retaliate by undercutting Royal Dutch/Shell's prices in India. As Royal Dutch/Shell responded with its own price-cutting in India, the price war spread to the United States and then to Europe. The resulting industry-wide chaos forced some small companies out of business and reduced company profits.

Realizing that all the companies suffered and that none could hope to win a price war, the heads of Royal Dutch/Shell, Anglo-Persian, and Standard of New Jersey met at Achnacarry Castle, Scotland, to try to control and contain the oil glut. The resulting Achnacarry or As Is agreement of September 1928 established seven principles that served as a declaration of intent by which the companies sought to preserve markets and limit competition. Even though the principals were never fully implemented, they were tacitly accepted by the leading oil-producing companies and provided a standard of inter-firm cooperation that was recognized for more than three decades.

The Achnacarry agreement rested on the premise that excessive competition had led to tremendous overproduction with destructive rather than constructive effects. The "as is" provisions embodied in the seven principles meant simply that no company had to fear incursions into its markets. The most important of the seven principles embodied the acceptance by the participants of the then present distribution of markets and proportionate increase in future production. Other principles stressed the necessity of adding new facilities only as needed to supply the increased needs of consumers, of maintaining for each producing area the financial advantage of its geographic location, and of preventing surplus production in one area from upsetting the price structure of any other area.

A major element of the agreement was the maintenance of U.S. prices as the basis for world market prices. The three companies adopted the *Gulf plus* pricing system for crude oil, whereby the price for oil delivered anywhere in the world was equal to the price of crude oil in the Gulf of Mexico market plus the cost of transportation if the oil had been shipped from the Gulf, no matter what its actual origin. The concept of *phantom freight* was employed to equalize delivery prices, despite differentials in transportation costs and between high-cost U.S. oil and low-cost foreign oil.

By 1930, however, it was clear that the Achnacarry agreement was insufficient to stabilize the world market. The U.S. producers were unable to fix prices or to establish exports quotas. The agreement did not cover the entire industry, and Russian and Rumanian exports were proving especially troublesome. There developed a number of important producing and marketing companies that were not bound by the agreement's principles. By undercutting the agreed prices, these outsiders could benefit from the Achnacarry arrangements.

Accordingly, three further agreements were negotiated between 1930 and 1934. Each of these agreements—the Memorandum for European Markets, the Heads of Agreement for Distribution, and the Draft Memorandum of Principles—had the objective of dividing local or national markets among the Achnacarry signatories and other leading multinational oil firms. All three of the agreements attempted, in an increasingly specific fashion, to fix quotas, to make adjustments for under- and over-trading by participants, to establish prices and other conditions of sale, and to create guidelines for dealing with outsiders.

The Memorandum for European Markets of January 20, 1930, attempted to stabilize the international industry through numerous local agreements rather than through a worldwide arrangement as had been attempted at Achnacarry. Under the terms of the memorandum, the companies were able to hold negotiations toward reducing Rumanian production. The willingness of the Rumanian producers to limit exports, however, depended upon the maintenance of a firm free on board (FOB) Gulf price, and their cooperation was withdrawn when members of the U.S. Export Association proved unable to fix prices.

On December 15, 1932, the Heads of Agreement for Distribution was adopted by Socony-Vacuum, Standard (NJ), Anglo Persian, Royal Dutch/Shell, Gulf, Atlantic Refining Company, and Texas Company. The Heads of Agreement for Distribution allowed the quota provision of Achnacarry to be applied more flexibly, so as to remedy the problems of fixing prices and sharing markets that had arisen when outsiders entered local marketing arrangements. Detailed provisions determined how much each participant would reduce its production quotas in local markets to allow for the output of outsiders, such as the Rumanian producers, and thereby prevent local gluts.

The 1932 agreement was to apply to the supply (production plus exports) and distribution of crude and refined oil in every country and area of the world, with the exception of the United States. Once again, agreements were negotiated with Russian and Rumanian producers to limit their exports and set their prices at levels established by the local marketing arrangements. To a greater degree than ever before, the Heads of Agreement for Distribution coordinated world supply agreements with local marketing arrangements.

Control over world production was maintained until the 1933 world depression combined with expanding U.S. production from the newly discovered East Texas fields to cause the fall of the U.S. Gulf price. A growing resistance to local marketing agreements based on "as is" principles developed, and Rumanian producers refused to cooperate with any type of production limitation agreement.

By 1934, U.S. prices had been raised and Royal Dutch/Shell, Standard (NJ), and Anglo-Persian had tightened their control over production in Venezuela and in the Middle East. On January 1, 1934, the Draft Memorandum of Principles was signed. It essentially restated the as-is principles contained in the previous agreements but provided even more detailed rules for quota adjustments and, for the first time, specified standards for local price determinations.

The Draft Memorandum was the final and the longest lived of the prewar international understandings between the major oil companies. It was formally discontinued in 1938, but the Gulf-plus price system continued to prevail until the mid-1950s. Except to the extent that they prevented a recurrence of price wars among the major oil companies, none of the agreements proved particularly effective in preserving the structure of the world petroleum trade.

Challenge and Response

In adherence to the provisions of the Red Line agreement of 1928, the members of the Iraq Petroleum Company were limiting their operations only to those undertaken through the IPC. Although the Red Line agreement provided against independent action by the members of the IPC, it could not prevent outsiders from seeking concessions within the areas of the red line. While a number of outside companies tried, and sometimes obtained, concessions within the territory of the red line, a greater challenge to IPC control was posed by Standard Oil of California's (SoCal) concession for the islands of Bahrain.

Frank Holmes had first obtained the Bahrain concession in the mid-1920s. After the concession was rejected by both Anglo-Persian and Standard Oil of New Jersey, Holmes was able to sell an option on it to Gulf. Gulf, however, after signing the Red Line agreement, as unable to develop the concession and sold it to Standard Oil of California in 1928. Oil was found in Bahrain in 1931, and exports began in 1933.

By offering King Ibn Saud of Saudi Arabia fifty thousand pounds of gold in 1933, an amount substantially more than that offered by the IPC, SoCal obtained a Saudi concession for 360,000 square miles, with a duration of sixty-six years. The specter of uncontrolled oil upsetting marketing arrangements and destabilizing prices in Europe and East Asia emerged again. Both collectively and individually, for almost seven years Anglo-Iranian, Standard (NJ), and Royal Dutch/Shell tried to get permission from the rest of the IPC to negotiate a separate agreement with Standard Oil of California for the controlled disposition of the oil from the Bahraini and Saudi concessions. The other members steadfastly refused, however, to suspend the provisions of the agreement. In essence, the 1928 agreement had backfired—although its intent was to limit competition among the IPC members, it instead prevented them from precluding competition by outsiders.

The members of the IPC had feared the impact of Standard Oil of California's production on world markets largely because SoCal had previously relied on Socony-Vacuum to market its oil products in the Far East. Since SoCal had no marketing facilities of its own, it was feared that a price war would occur as the firm sought to establish a market position. These fears were eased, however, in July 1936, when Standard Oil of California and Texas Company established Caltex, a jointly-owned company. Under this arrangement, Texas Company was to receive a 50 percent interest in SoCal's concessions in Saudi Arabia and in Bahrain, and SoCal gained a 50 percent interest in Texas Company's Far Eastern marketing facilities. This arrangement guaranteed the fusion of interests between the two companies, as Texas Company, which was historically short of crude oil, gained a firm source of supply, and SoCal acquired the marketing ability it had always lacked. The rest of the oil industry benefited also, for the assured markets for its new oil would reduce the likelihood of SoCal's attempting to penetrate established markets by cutting prices.

This newfound equilibrium was disturbed, after World War II, when it became evident that Saudi reserves were greater than Caltex's markets. Caltex was able to market in its outlets east of Suez only twelve to fifteen thousand barrels per day (b/d). This was less than 15 percent of Saudi capacity in 1941, and far less after new fields were discovered in 1945 and 1947. Owing to King Saud's desire for greater royalty payments, which meant increased production, Caltex was unable to leave the oil in the ground. The major companies feared that a flood of cheap Arabian oil—which was selling at about 90¢ per barrel in 1946, as compared to the lowest comparable U.S. Gulf price of $1.28—would upset world markets. Accordingly, discussions were begun between Standard Oil of California and Texas Company on the one hand, and Standard Oil of New Jersey and Socony-Vacuum on the other. An agreement was reached in principle in December 1946, by which Standard (NJ) and Socony-Vacuum would receive a 30 percent and 10 percent interest, respectively, in the Arabian American Oil Company (Aramco), which held the Caltex Saudi concession, and its Trans-Arabian Pipe Line Company (Tapline).

To join Aramco, however, both companies had to be exempted from the Red Line agreement. Negotiations with the other IPC members on this matter lasted until late in 1948, when it was decided to make the agreement less restrictive. IPC members would no longer have to share rights acquired within the area of the red line with other members. In return, Standard Oil of New Jersey promised a long-term contract to buy Anglo-Persian crude oil from Iran and Kuwait. Likewise, Royal Dutch/Shell was appeased by promises of long-term contracts from Mobil, and Gulbenkian and CFP were persuaded by the offer of Standard (NJ) to expand substantially Iraqi production. Caltex, which had previously been unable to market its oil west of Suez owing to the "as is" agreements, now could move its output through the marketing outlets of Standard Oil of New Jersey and Socony-Mobil. The companies in turn, avoided a potentially harmful price rivalry and managed to maintain their market positions.

Another joint venture had been established in Kuwait. In 1927, when Gulf had initially gained the concession for Bahrain from Frank Holmes, it also acquired the concession for Kuwait. Since Kuwait was outside the area of the red line, Gulf kept the concession and in 1933 joined in equal partnership with Anglo-Persian to form the Kuwait Oil Company. Each company explicitly promised the other that Kuwaiti oil would not be used to "upset or injure" the other's "trade or marketing position directly or indirectly at any time or place," in keeping with the "as is" provisions entailed in the 1932 Heads of Agreement for Distribution.[3] Under long-term sales contracts, Gulf agreed to provide Royal Dutch/Shell with over 1.5 billion barrels of Kuwaiti oil over a twenty-two year period and Anglo-Persian agreed to supply Standard Oil of New Jersey with 1.3 billion barrels over a twenty year period from either its Kuwaiti or Iranian production. In a 1947 contract with Shell, it was established that should Gulf use Kuwaiti oil to increase its share of any Eastern hemisphere market at Shell's expense, Gulf's deliveries to Shell would be reduced by an equal amount. Since Gulf and Shell also had agreed to share equally all the profits earned from their Kuwaiti operations, any attempt at price cutting by Gulf would only harm its own profits.

A similar long-term sales contract had been arranged between Anglo-Persian and both Socony-Vacuum and Standard (NJ) for the marketing of Anglo-Persian's Iranian oil. Like the purchase and sales agreement for its Kuwaiti oil, this too provided for the supply of large quantities of oil over long periods of time and contained restrictive provisions whereby Standard and Socony agreed to limit their sales to areas where they had already established a market position. The marketing arrangements for crude oil from Kuwait and Iran are both illustrative of the use of long-term supply contracts through which the major oil companies channelled large quantities of excess crude oil into world markets.

The Exercise of Control

By the late 1930s, the pattern of control over Middle East production and marketing had been firmly established by seven or eight companies. These multinational firms dominated all aspects of the oil industry and made the entry of smaller firms difficult. The use of joint-operating companies to conduct exploration, development, production, transportation, and sales intertwined the financial and equity interests of firms. This pattern of control limited competition and established a mutually advantageous arrangement whereby companies both long and short on crude oil could benefit from one anothers' reserves and marketing positions.

Although the outbreak of World War II temporarily interrupted the expansion of the oil industry, most companies survived the war intact. After the war, the lifting of import quotas by major consuming nations created new markets, and the growing conversion from coal to oil led to an increase in oil demand that would eventually produce an elevenfold increase in noncommunist consumption from 1948 to 1972. In addition, decolonialization meant the emergence of new countries welcoming the oil companies as a source of capital investment for the development of their oil resources. Indeed, the immediate postwar period was particularly favorable for the international oil industry: the major companies exercised a high degree of influence over the market, profits were high, and the companies were, more or less, able to develop and expand with few impediments. The long-term sales contracts of crude oil complemented the joint ventures of the 1930s and entrenched the position held by the majors throughout the 1940s and into the 1950s.

The extent of control the companies achieved over the industry was exemplified by their ability to circumvent the Iranian nationalization of Anglo-Iranian's assets in 1951. A nationalistic Iranian National Assembly, the Majlis, demanded that Anglo-Iranian adopt a fifty-fifty profit-sharing agreement, under the terms of which the host country's share of profits from production rose to 50 percent, a significant increase over the 12.5 percent royalty rate then common in the Middle East. First instituted by Venezuela in 1948, "fifty-fifty" spread to Saudi Arabia and other Middle East producers by 1950. When Anglo-Iranian offered a supplemental agreement instead of a fifty-fifty one, the Majlis rejected the offer. In the militant atmosphere that followed, the Prime Minister was killed early in 1951 and Dr. Mohammed Mossadegh, a strong advocate of nationalization, was elected by the Majlis to the post. Anglo-Iranian was nationalized in May 1951, and the National Iranian Oil Company (NIOC) was established to produce and market Iranian oil.

The power of the major oil companies was such, however, that a collective boycott of Iranian oil by the eight majors (including the largest French firm, CFP) was almost completely effective. Unable to penetrate the established markets of the majors, Iranian oil exports fell from over $400 million in 1950 to less than $2 million for the entire period of July 1951 to August 1953. Although Iran accounted for nearly one-fifth of world exports in 1950, the oil companies easily compensated for the loss of Iranian oil by increasing production elsewhere, mainly in Kuwait, Iraq, and Saudi Arabia. In August 1953, Mossadegh was overthrown in a CIA-supported coup, and the Shah was returned to the throne.

After the overthrow of Mossadegh, the majors had to alter the production patterns that had developed during the boycott of nationalized Iranian oil.

A consortium including all eight major multinational oil firms was established to buy oil from NIOC. Although NIOC retained legal control of Iranian production, the consortium members regained effective control by means of their regulation of daily operations, their management of the Iranian fields, and their exclusive control of world markets. Anglo-Iranian (which became British Petroleum in 1954) held a 40 percent share in the consortium, while Shell got 14 percent, CFP 6 percent, and Standard Oil of California, Texas, Standard Oil of New Jersey, Gulf, and Mobil each received 7 percent. Under pressure by the U.S. Department of Justice, the majors were forced to admit nine independent U.S. companies to the consortium, but the majors managed to limit the independents' share to 5 percent. The majors wanted to exclude, or at least to limit, the independents' share because, with no secure market position, these firms were likely to try to penetrate established markets by cutting prices. This would mean a fresh challenge to the market and the pricing control of the majors.

At the same time, the eight majors in the consortium also negotiated a participants agreement that set the terms under which they would buy Iranian oil and restrict production to avoid a glut on world markets. In this fashion, Iranian production was limited by penalizing any company that lifted more oil than the secret agreement allowed. A similar off-take agreement restricted production from Saudi fields. In this way, Middle East production was carefully orchestrated so as not to exceed forecasted world demand, and a careful, and profitable, equilibrium was maintained.

The majors' success at controlling the world market, however, was to help contribute to the disintegration of the industry's structure. The high profit levels of the industry attracted independent companies eager to cash-in on growing world demand. Concessions were available in newly independent countries, such as Libya, Algeria, and Nigeria, which were eager to tap their unused oil wealth. These conditions, combined with the willingness of the new companies to assume greater risks and offer more generous terms than the majors, led to a growth in world production. By the late 1950s, there was a glut of oil on world markets, as control over the international oil industry slipped from the grasp of the majors.

Evidence of the declining power of the majors was evident in their share of production. The 92 percent of non-Communist (excluding U.S.) world production controlled by the majors in 1955 slid to 84 percent by 1960 and fell to 76 percent by 1965. The world price structure, previously controlled by the majors, began to crumble, as new crude-oil production rose, and as the majors' hold on markets slipped, independents began agressively to cut prices. The rise of the independents, the slipping prices for crude, and the majors' response—to cut prices—set the stage for the creation of OPEC and the revolution that wrested control of the oil industry from the major companies.

Table 4-1
Ownership of Middle East Oil Concessions, 1960s
(percent)

Concession	Company								
	BP (Anglo-Iranian)	Exxon (Standard NJ)	CFP	Gulf	Shell	Texaco	SoCal	Mobil (Socony-Vacuum)	Share of Concession Held by Eight Majors
Abu Dhabi Marine Areas	66.67		33.3						100
Abu Dhabi Petroleum Company (United Arab Emirates)	23.75	11.875	23.75		23.75			11.875	95
Aramco		30				30	30	10	100
Bahrain Petroleum Company						50	50		100
Iranian Consortium	40	7	6	7	14	7	7	7	95
Iraq Petroleum Company	23.75	11.875	23.75		23.75			11.875	95
Kuwait Oil Company	50			50					100
Qatar Petroleum Company	23.75	11.875	23.75		23.75			11.875	95

Source: Compiled from annual reports of the various companies.

Notes

1. Statement to House of Commons, July 17, 1913. Cited in *International Petroleum Cartel*, Staff Report of the Federal Trade Commission, submitted to the Senate Judiciary Committee, Subcommittee on Monopoly, 82d Cong., 2d Sess., August 1952, p. 49.

2. Federal Trade Commission, *International Petroleum Cartel*, p. 66.

3. Ibid, pp. 131–132.

5

State-Owned Oil Companies and OPEC

Producer Cooperation in the Forties and Fifties

Although it was the sequence of events from 1973 to 1974 that brought OPEC to the forefront of the world petroleum scene, the organization had already been in existence for over a decade. While the extent to which the producing nations were to seize control over their production and pricing could not have been foreseen at the time of OPEC's creation in 1960, the majors' absolute control had, in fact, been gradually slipping over to the OPEC nations for over a decade. It took the drama of the Arab producer's oil embargo and OPEC's unilateral price-hikes to convince the world—and the oil companies—that the majors were no longer in command of the world petroleum market.

The ability of the OPEC nations to control petroleum operations within their borders represents a drastic change in the status of the producer nations in relation to the oil companies. Historically, the granting of concession rights gave a company control over all aspects of petroleum activities. Payments to the producing countries were nominal, countries had no voice in the rate of exploitation of their reserves, and they did not participate in upstream exploration and production—much less downstream refining and marketing—operations.

Venezuela was the first country in the postwar period to assert that producers should realize greater benefits from and exert more influence over their petroleum activities. Beginning in 1943, Venezuela cancelled all existing concessions and raised the royalty rate to 16 2/3 percent on the granting of new concessions. Five years later, Perez Alfonso, Venezuela's development minister, introduced a new tax requiring the companies to pay 50 percent of all profits to the Venezuelan government. Realizing that fifty-fifty profit-sharing made Venezuelan oil more dear than crude oil from other nations, Venezuela encouraged other producers to adopt similar laws. In 1949, Venezuela sent an official delegation to Iran, Iraq, Kuwait, and Saudi Arabia to establish contact with producers in the Middle East and discuss ways to maintain closer and more regular communication.

The Venezuelan consultations proved to have an influence on the Middle East producers. In December 1950, Saudi Arabia rejected the traditional royalty of a fixed-fee per unit of production, adopted its own fifty-fifty profit-sharing, and instituted an income tax for the first time. By 1951, some form of the fifty-fifty profit split had been adopted by all the governments in the Middle East.

The fifty-fifty clauses were accepted benignly by the companies operating in the Middle East. In reality, fifty-fifty profit sharing was misnamed because all royalties, rental fees, and other payments owed by the companies were deducted from the 50 percent share of profits to be paid to the Middle East governments. The companies were willing to accept the fifty-fifty arrangement because they were allowed (and encouraged) by the U.S. government to count the additional payments as foreign income taxes, which were deductible from their total U.S. tax bill. By means of this tax credit, any increases in payments to the producing governments was simply passed-on to the U.S. Treasury. The ability of the companies to pass-on extra taxes enabled them to satisfy the financial demands of the countries at no additional cost to themselves, while maintaining control over the industry and keeping high profits.

There were other examples in the 1950s of movement toward greater cooperation among producing countries. In light of the then-current conflict between the major companies and Iran following the Iranian nationalization of Anglo-Iranian in 1951, Iraq and Saudi Arabia signed the first formal agreement of cooperation between two petroleum exporting nations in June 1953. They agreed to exchange information and meet periodically to discuss petroleum policies. In addition, to improve their bargaining positions vis-a-vis the oil firms, Iraq and Saudi Arabia began to insert best-terms clauses into their concessionary agreements. These clauses enabled host governments to discuss contract revisions with the concessionaires should neighboring countries receive better contract terms. Best-terms clauses soon spread to other Middle East producers in the early 1950s.

Despite the spread of fifty-fifty profit sharing and best-terms clauses, contact and cooperation between the producing nations were limited in the 1940s and 1950s. By the end of the 1950s, however, an increase in the number of independent oil firms indicated a loosening of the majors' ability to dominate the industry. The rise in world production outside of the multinationals' control and the emergence of a world oil glut provoked the majors to cut prices, thereby sparking the creation of OPEC in 1960.

The Role of the Independents

Beginning in the immediate postwar period, there was a rapid growth in the number of independent oil firms. Worldwide, from 1953 to 1972, more than three hundred private companies and over fifty government companies entered or undertook major expansion in the industry. While there had been only six U.S. companies other than the majors conducting overseas exploration in 1945, there were some thirty with foreign exploration rights a decade later.

There were several conditions in the postwar period that enabled the independents to enter the industry. The U.S. oil industry was mature. New exploration opportunities beckoned overseas. The emergence of many newly independent nations led to production where the majors, who already controlled large source of supply, had not sought concessions. These nations often were eager to expand their oil production to finance their economic growth and welcomed the rapid development of their oil resources by the independents. The willingness of the new companies to assume high risks and to provide more generous terms than those offered by the majors enabled the new producer nations to grant large numbers of concessions and to expand output rapidly.

The availability of new concessions gave the independents access to large amounts of oil. Many of the independents chose to market their newly acquired oil directly, rather than rely on the marketing facilities of the majors, and were competing with the majors both upstream and downstream. Owing to the high fixed-costs of entering the industry, it was incrementally profitable for the new firms to sell as much crude oil as possible, even at lowered prices, so they expanded output rapidly and cut prices to penetrate markets. Growing world oil demand facilitated the efforts of the independents to market their production without relying on the distribution networks of the majors.

The increased activity by the independents meant large increases in the volume of petroleum that moved outside the integrated channels controlled by the majors. The adoption of mandatory import quotas in the United States in March 1959 effectively severed the United States from the world market and forced the independents to compete in European and Japanese markets. In addition, an increasing volume of Soviet oil was being exported to Western markets. The growing supply of crude oil on world markets exerted a steady downward pressure on prices in the late 1950s.

The excess supply of crude oil and the price-cutting actions by the independents had already forced the majors to sell their oil below the posted price. As the oil glut worsened, and the difference between the posted prices and the discounted prices continued to grow larger, the majors' profit margins decreased. Unable to control world oil production, the multinationals felt that their only recourse was to cut posted prices. In February 1959, the posted price was lowered by eighteen cents per barrel, and was followed in August 1960 by a further reduction of eight to ten cents per barrel. The oil producing nations reacted to these cuts with anger and dismay. Previously, these countries had been insulated from the decline in market prices because their royalties and taxes were based on the posted prices, not on the discounted market price. Now they were faced with a price cut that would translate into a loss of government revenues of billions of dollars during the 1960s.

The Birth of OPEC

Reaction by the oil producing nations came swiftly. After the price cut of February 1959, the First Arab Oil Congress convened in Cairo in April, with Iran and Venezuela attending as observers. The Congress provided a forum for the producers to express their dissatisfaction with the price cuts. At the initiative of Venezuela's Perez Alfonso, an Oil Consulation Commission was created with the aim of achieving cooperation among its members. The commission recommended that the posted or tax-reference price on exports be stabilized; that the governments' tax takes on exports be increased; and that the companies seek the approval of producing governments for future price changes. The commission proved to be short-lived, however, owing to internal differences among the members. Nevertheless, producer cooperation had been tried, and the roots of OPEC have often been traced to the First Arab Oil Congress.

Shortly after the multinational companies again cut prices in August 1960, representatives of Iran, Kuwait, Saudi Arabia, Iraq, and Venezuela gathered in Baghdad. This historic meeting from September 10 through 14 resulted in the establishment of OPEC. Although the loss of revenues and income resulting from the price reductions was an important factor behind OPEC's creation, the unilateral nature of the price changes was equally significant. National sovereignty, Shah Mohammad Riza Pahlavi of Iran argued, and ownership of natural resources necessitated that the producer states exercise control over pricing decisions.

OPEC was established to coordinate and unify the petroleum policies of the producer countries. OPEC's immediate objectives were outlined at the Bagdad meeting in a resolution demanding that prices be kept steady and free from unnecessary fluctuations, that prices be restored to the levels prevailing before the reductions, and that the companies consult with the host governments on future price changes.

OPEC, however, despite its brave rhetoric at birth, was still very much a foundling on the world petroleum scene. The disparity between the power wielded by the majors over petroleum activities, and the role of the host governments in the development of their oil resources is striking. In 1960, these five nations owned 67 percent of the world's oil reserves, provided almost 90 percent of the oil in international trade, and were the source of 38 percent of total world production. Yet the eight majors controlled 92 percent of OPEC's production and determined the rate at which the oil was lifted, the price at which it was marketed, and the consumer to whom the oil would eventually be sold.

Early Successes

OPEC remained quiescent until its fourth conference, held in Geneva in June 1962, where it prepared to demand a greater share of the oil companies' profits. A study commissioned by OPEC in 1961 estimated that 1956–1960 the average net earnings on net assets of the major Middle East oil-producing concessions (less price discounts) were 71 percent for Iran, 62 percent for Iraq, 61 percent for Saudi Arabia, and 114 percent for Qatar.[1] The OPEC nations felt that they deserved a greater share of the profits. Accordingly, at the June 1962 conference, they resolved to ask the companies to eliminate marketing expense allowances, to establish royalty expensing, and to raise posted prices to pre-August 1960 levels.

The dispute over the companies' practice of deducting a marketing expense— a percentage from taxable revenues to account for the cost of marketing petroleum—was not a new one. In the original fifty-fifty profit-sharing agreements marketing expenses had been set at 2 percent of posted prices, and through the use of best-terms clauses the companies had been pressured to reduce this amount to 2 percent by 1960. Negotiations began with the oil companies in 1962 toward its elimination. OPEC considered the expense to be a fictitious one, since the bulk of crude-oil production was marketed through long-term contracts or between parents and subsidiaries and, therefore, incurred no brokerage fees or other marketing costs. A settlement was reached in 1964, when the allowable deductible amount was reduced to 0.5 cents per barrel from 1.7 cents per barrel. Although not a full OPEC victory, it added significantly to their revenues.

Negotiations on the issue of royalty expensing were also begun in 1962. Since the Middle East governments instituted income taxes and fifty-fifty profit-sharing in the early 1950s, the oil companies had treated royalties like taxes. That is, they would include royalty payments, which in the Middle East averaged about 12.5 percent, as part of the 50 percent of the net revenues they owed, thereby reducing revenues earned by the producer governments. The OPEC nations argued that royalties were legitimate payments in themselves and should be treated independently from company profits to adequately compensate the owners for the depletion of a non-renewable resource. Under a system of royalty expensing, royalties would be treated as an operating cost and deducted from gross income before determining the net revenues to which the 50 percent tax would be applied.

After fifteen months of negotiation, a compromise was reached. The companies agreed to adopt the principle of royalty expensing and, in exchange, were given discount allowances off the posted price for heavy crude oils. Although owing to the discount allowance the OPEC producers received less of an increase in revenues than if full royalty expensing had taken place, the compromise settlement did add more than $100 million annually to Middle East treasuries from 1964 to 1966. In 1966-1968, further negotiations were held on this same issue. With the improvement of marketing conditions as a result of tightening world supply, the oil companies agreed to phase-out both the tax-deductible royalty and discounts for heavier crude oils over a period of several years.

Negotiations toward the final objective of the 1962 OPEC conference, the raising of posted prices, were not as successful as the first two. Talks began in 1962, but the companies steadfastly refused to restore posted prices to their pre-August 1960 level. The majors consistently—and successfully—argued that increasing prices at a time of oversupply and intense price competition would result in reduced sales and loss of markets. Posted prices did, however, remain steady for the entire decade, and, although the market continued to weaken, the producer nations were insulated from the growing disparity between the posted prices and world market prices that resulted from discounting. This did represent a victory for OPEC, as the stabilization of prices was one of the objectives set in 1960.

In both 1965–1966 and 1966–1967, the OPEC nations attempted joint-production programming as a way to stabilize prices. They hoped to achieve control over production by preventing the companies from playing one producer country off against another, as the majors successfully did in response to the Iranian nationalization, when additional production from neighboring countries was used to compensate for the shortfall. Both attempts failed owing to the emphasis placed by some members on market shares rather than prices, the differences over a mutually acceptable prorationing scheme, and the lack of cooperation by the companies.

By the end of 1964 there had been some achievements: royalty expensing had been adopted; marketing allowances had been substantially reduced; and government revenues per barrel, after declining 1957–1961, had started to rise by 1963, while oil company earnings per barrel continued a downward decline to 1970. By June 1962, OPEC had gained three new members—Qatar, Libya, and Indonesia (to be followed by Abu Dhabi in 1967, Algeria in 1969, Nigeria in 1971, Ecuador in 1973, and Gabon in 1975)—thus adding to its credibility as a collective voice for the Third World oil-producing nations.

Despite these minor successes, however, the oil companies remained very much in control of the world oil industry, and further actions by OPEC during its first decade of existence proved to be inconclusive. As was evident from OPEC's failed attempts at prorationing in the mid-1960s, OPEC had not yet discovered the strategy, or the means, to control the market.

OPEC's sixteenth conference, in Vienna in June 1968, however, produced the program that would serve as a blueprint for the exporting nations' long-range strategy toward the oil companies. In the "Declaratory Statement of Petroleum Policy of Member Countries" OPEC outlined its intent to seek ownership and control over production and prices. Among the ten points in the declaratory statement, was the recommendation that the producers endeavor "to explore for and develope their hydrocarbon resources directly," and at the minimum, "retain the greatest measure possible of participation in and control over all aspects of operations."[2] Further points declared that, should changing events warrant it, concession agreements should be revised and governments could acquire ownership of producing companies. Under the statement, prices would be set by host governments and could be adjusted to compensate for declining terms of trade. Although the statement attracted little attention at the time, it served as a broad policy outline for OPEC members.

The buyers market in oil that prevailed for most of the 1960s had helped keep OPEC weak. A change in market forces in the late 1960s and early 1970s, however, strengthened OPEC's position. Under these conditions, the willingness of Libya to challenge the oil companies in 1970 provided OPEC with the opportunity to put the proposed principles of 1968 into practice.

The Libyan Strategy

Libya's confrontation with the oil companies over prices was a decisive catalyst for change in the Middle East. Libya's ability to do battle with the companies resulted from her practice, begun after World War II, of giving independent companies access to concessions, as a means of preventing domination by the majors. By 1970, independents were lifting more than 50 percent of Libya's crude-oil, compared to an average of 15 percent for the other OPEC countries.

In September 1968, Colonel Maummar al-Qadaffi, an Arab nationalist, overthrew King Idris of Libya. Qadaffi was determined to raise oil prices and end what he considered injurious overlifting of Libyan oil. He demanded conservation safeguards, a price increase of forty cents per barrel, and an increase in the tax rate from 50 percent to 55 percent. When the twenty-one companies operating in Libya refused to meet his demand, Qadaffi adopted a policy of confrontation.

There were several circumstances working in Qadaffi's favor. The 1960s had seen the growing dependence of the industrialized nations on imported crude oil. The demand for OPEC oil alone had increased almost 300 percent from 1960 to 1970. Libyan oil, owing to its low sulphur content and its proximity to European markets, was particularly desirable and accounted for one quarter of Western Europe's oil needs by 1970. Immediate market conditions also helped the Libyan position. Short-haul Libyan crude oil already held a strong market advantage after the Suez Canal was closed by the 1967 Arab–Israeli war, and this advantage was further strengthened when the Trans-Arabian Pipeline (Tapline), which daily carried 500,000 barrels of Saudi oil to the Mediterranean, was closed in May 1970. A shortage of tankers and the interruption of Nigerian production in 1970 by the Biafran war made shipments of Libyan crude oil even more vital at a time when European demand was exceeding industry expectations. Finally, Libya was able to take advantage of the long-existing rivalry between the majors and the independents.

In June 1970, the Libyan government informed the Occidental Petroleum Company, an independent firm working in Libya, that its production would be reduced from 800,000 to 500,000 barrels per day. In August, Occidental's production was again cut, to 440,000 b/d, or only 55 percent of its former production. Qadaffi had chosen Occidental because of its vulnerability to cutbacks: it was dependent on Libyan oil for almost one-third of its total earnings, had no alternate source of supply, and would be unable to fulfill its contractual commitment without suffering heavy losees. The seven majors refused to come to

Occidental's aid and left it no choice but to capitulate. In September, Occidental agreed to raise the posted price by thirty cents per barrel, rising to forty cents over the next five years, and also accepted a 5 percent increase in the tax rate, retroactive to 1965.

Qadaffi then turned on the Oasis group, a consortium of three independents (Amerada, Continental, and Marathon), and Royal Dutch/Shell. The independents were largely dependent on Libyan oil and yielded, but Royal Dutch/ Shell refused to concede. In September 1970, Qadaffi suspended all of Shell's Libyan production. By this time, only the large majors were refusing Qadaffi's demands. Soon, however, Texaco and SoCal, followed by the other U.S. majors and lastly by Royal Dutch/Shell, acceded to the price and tax increases. There was no alternative for the majors, who were faced with the possibility of nationalization and the takeover of their concessions by either a national oil company or by independents.

The Libyan settlement proved to be a turning point in the petroleum industry. By restricting production and increasing the tax rate, Libya broke the twenty-year tradition of fifty-fifty profit-sharing, proved the authority of the host governments to unilaterally set prices, and forced the companies to accept the principle of retroactive price increases. In October 1970, the oil companies of the Iraq Petroleum Company raised prices on their own initiative. Negotiations with Iran then began through the Iranian consortium, in which all the majors and several independents were represented. The settlement reached with Iran allowed a price hike of nine cents per barrel for heavy crude oils, and an increase in the tax rate to 55 percent. Negotiations with other oil producers led to settlements at similar terms.

Tripoli and Teheran

Emboldened by their successes, the OPEC nations in December 1970, at their twenty-first conference, in Caracas, called for a minimum 55 percent income tax rate, an increase in posted prices, and the elimination of deductions of royalties from income taxes and marketing allowances from posted prices. At the conference, OPEC also decided to hold negotiations with the companies on a regional basis, with the nations of the Persian Gulf, the Mediterranean, and Venezuela and Indonesia combining to constitute separate regions. Their aim was to achieve a uniform pricing structure based on the highest posted price received by a member country, taking into account gravity and geographic differentials. If the companies refused, the OPEC nations agreed to act unilaterally on their demands. As is evident by the negotiating stance reached at Caracas, OPEC had begun a new strategy, more in line with that outlined in their 1968 declaratory statement, through which they intended to assume the prerogative of price setting. In effect, a compulsory best-terms pricing provision was going to be enforced.

To strengthen their bargaining position, the oil companies decided to negotiate collectively with the producers.[3] Mindful of their recent experiences in

Libya, they also developed a safety-net agreement in which all the companies would share crude oil with any company that had its supply reduced or cut-off by Libya during the negotiations. The twenty-three companies involved in the negotiations sought one comprehensive agreement covering all OPEC members, or at least simultaneous negotiations with the Persian Gulf producers and with the Mediterranean producers to prevent a leapfrogging of demands between the two groups for higher taxes and prices. OPEC refused, and separate talks were scheduled for Teheran and Tripoli.

When the negotiations opened in Teheran on July 19, 1971, the Persian Gulf governments requested an increase in prices averaging forty-five cents per barrel in 1971, and increasing to eighty cents by 1975. The companies balked, and further negotiations led to a minimum demand of thirty cents for 1971, rising to fifty-three cents by 1975. At that point, the talks broke down. The OPEC nations met at their twenty-third conference on February 3 and resolved that, if the companies failed to negotiate a settlement by February 15, each country would then unilaterally set new prices and taxes on its oil. On February 15, the companies conceded. Posted prices rose immediately by thirty cents per barrel, and would rise an average of fifty cents by 1975 to account for inflation. The companies also reiterated their acceptance of a 55 percent tax rate and agreed to eliminate all special allowances. In return, the companies were promised that there would be no leapfrogging for better terms, nor would there be production cutbacks aimed at obtaining higher prices for the next five years.

Negotiations were then held with the Mediterranean producers at Tripoli.[4] An agreement was signed on April 2, 1971, with terms that leapfrogged over those reached at Teheran. Like the Teheran agreement it was to be for five years, with annual adjustments for inflation, but the price increases were greater, and a special premium for Libyan crude oil was included.

Less than six months later, the OPEC countries acted to implement another principle outlined in the 1968 statement and reiterated at the Caracas conference. To protect their purchasing power, they resolved that posted prices be adjusted to compensate for unfavorable changes in the "currency parities of the member countries." After the U.S. decision on August 15, 1971, to float the dollar, followed by its subsequent devaluation, the OPEC countries resolved in September to seek compensation for their loss in real income per barrel. The issue of parity was settled easily, as the companies agreed in Geneva in January 1972, and in June (after a second devaluation of the dollar in February), to upwardly adjust the posted price and link it to a basket of currencies. The negotiations in Geneva completed the process begun at Teheran and Tripoli and gave the producer nations, for the first time, control over the price of their oil.

OPEC Power

It was not long, however, before OPEC called further negotiations on prices. The Persion Gulf producers had never been fully satisfied with the Teheran agreement, which had failed to foresee the advent of tightening supplies and the increase in market prices in mid-1973 to the point where they overtook posted prices. New negotiations began on October 8, 1973, with the OPEC producers demanding a doubling of prices. Negotiations adjourned October 12 to allow the companies to consult with their home governments, which subsequently rejected the increases. OPEC responded on October 16 with a unilateral price increase of 70 percent, raising the price of Saudi marker crude-oil from $3.01 to $5.12. The price increases went unchallenged, as the Arab producers (except Iraq) responded to the Yom Kippur war by adopting an oil embargo against the United States and the Netherlands. Production cutbacks ranging from 11 percent to 20 percent in the third and fourth quarters of 1973 tightened world supply, and sent market prices soaring to $20 per barrel for certain crude oils. The OPEC nations then announced further price increases, effective January 1, 1974, which raised the price of Saudi marker crude oil to $11.65. OPEC had dramatically asserted its right to determine its revenues through unilateral price changes.

While OPEC was asserting control over prices, it also began to assume a greater role in production, either through participation of nationalization, moving toward their eventual direct management of production by national oil companies. Algeria, as a result of its disputes with France, had nationalized 51 percent of all French petroleum assets and concessions in February 1971. Venezuela followed Algeria's initiative the following August by calling for 100 percent government ownership of the national oil industry by 1983. At the extraordinary conference in Beirut in September 1971, OPEC members were urged to act immediately to participate in existing concessions, under terms whereby the government share in producing companies would be gradually increased until full ownership was achieved. The Algerian nationalization of the oil industry signalled that the transfer of company control had begun.

In January 1972, Saudi Arabia's oil minister, Sheikh Ahmad Zaki Yamani began negotiations on behalf of Saudi Arabia, Kuwait, Qatar, and Abu Dhabi toward increased participation. As the negotiations dragged on, the four countries threatened to impose sanctions if the companies did not accept their increased participation. By the time an agreement was reached in October 1973, Libya had nationalized 51 percent of its British Petroleum (BP) concession and Iraq had taken-over 100 percent of the Iraq Petroleum Company. Under the October agreement, the four governments were to receive immediately a 25 percent equity share, which would increase to 51 percent by 1982. Compensation was to be based on updated book value, and a supplementary agreement signed in December set the price and established the percentage of the governments' share of *participation* crude oil (also called *bridging* or *buy-back* oil), which would be sold to the companies so they could fulfill their contractual obligations. Provisions were also made for *phase-in* oil, whereby the governments had the option of selling to the companies those quantities the governments and their agents were not able to market themselves.

The OPEC nations were not long satisfied with their share. Libya, which had nearly completed the 51 percent takeover of most fields by April 1974, was soon seeking 80 percent participation. Before the oil embargo was lifted in March 1974, Kuwait and Qatar became the first OPEC members to claim a 60 percent stake, and Kuwait, Saudi Arabia, and Venezuela announced their intent to reach 100 percent participation. By 1975, either through participation agreements or partial nationalization, control over production and exports rested in the producers' hands. Since then, their degree of ownership has continued to grow. By the end of 1980, Iran, Kuwait, Qatar, Saudi Arabia, and Bahrain had achieved 100 percent takeover, while Oman, Abu Dhabi, and Nigeria owned 60 percent. For most OPEC countries, and oil producers in general, as national skills, and experience grow, increased national ownership and control can be expected.

The emergence of the oil producing states as fully active and controlling actors by the mid-1970s was to have nearly as much impact (albeit a much quieter one) on the international petroleum industry as did the price and production revolution in the first half of the decade. The oil companies were able to adjust to OPEC's assumption of the responsibility for price-setting, largely because they were able to pass higher prices to retail markets. As the companies were forced to shift their profit centers downstream to refining and marketing, they realized that crude-oil ownership was no longer essential but, rather, that assured access to crude was becoming increasingly critical.

Participation by OPEC governments in production and the purchase of their participation crude by the companies, created a tripartite oil market in which the oil companies play a dual role as both the producers and purchasers of crude. The increasing use of service contracts, in which the oil firms operate as contractors for national oil companies, not only reflects the changed position of the companies, but also the redirection of their emphasis to obtaining access to crude in a period of unpredictable supply.

Another important change in the world petroleum industry has been the emergence of national oil companies and their expanded role in all aspects of the industry. Today, there are several hundred state petroleum companies, both consumer- and producer-owned, in over ninety countries. Although their existence is not new—two of the first postwar national oil companies were the National Iranian Oil Company, established in 1951, and Italy's Ente Nazionale Idrocarburi (ENI), established in 1953—their earlier role was largely a limited one. In the producing countries, they had done little more than gather information, carry out non-basic oil operations, and, in a few cases, hold responsibility for local marketing. It was only with the advent of government participation that state-owned oil companies in the producing nations gained access to crude that they could market directly on world markets. Even then, joint-venture agreements between national oil companies and major oil companies often consisted of little more than long-term contracts through which the multinationals bought the government's share of participation oil. Although by June 1979 all the OPEC countries had established national oil companies, these range, depending on the technological expertise of the country, from actual operating enterprises to mere holding companies.

Despite the widespread establishment of national oil companies, the major multinationals continue to market most of the world's oil. This pattern began to change in the late 1970s and the shift to producer marketing will not doubt accelerate in the 1980s. According to John Lichtblau, executive director of the Petroleum Industry Research Foundation in New York, the central actor in the petroleum market ". . . is [now] the national oil company—and most crude oil buyers will have to kook to it and accept its terms to obtain future supplies."[5] Lichtblau recorded that sales by state oil companies to commercial buyers had grown from under 1.5 million barrels per day (mb/d) in 1975, to 8 mb/d in 1980. As a result of the expanded trade by the national companies, the multinationals' supplies have become less assured, and they are often driven to seek extra crude in the spot market. As the national oil companies of the OPEC countries continue to expand downstream, the oil companies domination of these aspects of the industry will also be challenged, and the petroleum industry will become increasingly diverse in the areas of marketing, refining, shipping, and petrochemicals.

The OPEC revolution created a fluidity and diversity in the international petroleum industry that is in stark contrast to the tightly controlled, vertically integrated structure created by the major multinationals. Today, sales by a variety of both private- and state-owned companies, and even directly between governments, have meant a greater volume of oil moving outside of the pre-1973 channels of parent to subsidiary, and the long-term oil market has been supplemented by a short-term one. The increasing importance of spot-market sales and prices, the greater volatility of markets, and the uncertainty regarding future supply and price, are part of the evolution of the international petroleum industry as it moves further away from the tightly controlled and integrated industry of the past.

Notes

1. The study, by Arthur D. Little, was titled "Economic Aspects of the International Petroleum Industry, Report to the Organization of the Petroleum Exporting Countries," 2 vols. (Cambridge, Mass., Jan. 15, 1962). Figures cited are attributed as representative of the study by Zuhayr Mikdashiin, *The Community of Oil Exporting Countries: A Study in Governmental Cooperation* (Ithaca, New York: Cornell University Press, 1972), p. 141.

2. Resolution XVI.90, OPEC's Sixteenth Conference, June 24–25, 1968. Cited in Dankwart A. Rustow and John F. Mugno, *OPEC: Success and Prospects* (New York: Council on Foreign Relations, New York University Press, 1976), pp. 168–169.

3. Prior to negotiating collectively with OPEC, the U.S. oil companies requested, and received, clearance from the U.S. Justice Department and the U.S. State Department in order to avoid possible U.S. antitrust prosecution. The European companies did not have to worry about violating antitrust laws but did inform their home governments of their intention to negotiate collectively.

4. The Mediterranean producers included Nigeria, Libya, Algeria, Saudi Arabia, and Iran. Both Saudi Arabia and Iran participated in the Tripoli negotiations, in addition to the Teheran negotiations for the Persion Gulf producers, because Tapline gave them access to the Mediterranean. Nigeria joined OPEC just in time to participate in the Tripoli negotiations.

5. *Financial Times* (London), "State Corporations Flex Their Muscles," June 3, 1980, p. 4.

6   The Rotterdam Oil Market

Spot Markets

Spot markets, as an adjunct to contract sales and the integrated trade of the petroleum industry, have become more visible of late. In particular, their role in the oil trade was highlighted by soaring spot transactions and prices after the Iranian revolution in early 1979. The increasing decentralization of the world petroleum market and the volatility of prices in the 1970s have prompted consumers and producers to focus their attention on the spot market. Spot markets for both crude and oil products, however, have been operating at the margin of the petroleum industry for decades.

Tight control by the majors over the flow of oil through integrated channels from the wellhead, through refining and marketing, meant that prior to 1970, for the most part, there was no real open market for either crude or oil products. To a great extent, their sale was often just a matter of bookkeeping within the large multinational oil companies. In addition, the sale of oil through long-term, fixed-proced contracts precluded the operation of an open market for trade in oil.

Even today, the spot market is not a market in the usual sense, a place where buyers and sellers meet to conduct business. Instead, the participants are in cities around the world—London, Paris, New York, Tokyo, Milan, and Hamburg, to name a few—and all trading is conducted by telex and telephone. Nor is the Rotterdam market similar to an official bourse. As reported by the Bourse Study Group of the Commission of the European Communities which was established to examine this issue, the Rotterdam market has no membership registration, no official reporting of prices and volumes, no formal administrative oversight, nor any trading in futures—activities that usually characterize a bourse. Nevertheless, the Rotterdam market functions effectively as a free market for the day-to-day trading of contracts for physical delivery of crudes and petroleum products.

Development of the Rotterdam Market

Although several refining and terminalling areas, such as New York Harbor, the Caribbean, or the Far East trade centered in Singapore, serve centers for spot trades, it is the Rotterdam market that is most often identified as the heart of spot trading activity. Development of the Rotterdam market has its roots in the growth of the European refining industry after World War II, when most European governments and oil companies undertook refinery construction programs. The emphasis was upon refining within their borders, with less investment in Middle Eastern or Caribbean refinery centers. There were several advantages to be gained from such a program. By importing crude rather than products, large tankers could be used with significant economies of scale. Also, the foreign exchange shortage of the postwar period made it more economical to buy crude oil for refining in Europe, rather than pay the additional cost for refined oil. Finally, by building them close to the consuming centers, refineries could be designed to suit the specifications of local demand, notably a requirement for the heavy-oil that was needed in increasing volumes to generate electricity.

As postwar economies boomed, European refinery capacity rose from under 3 mb/d in 1948 to more than 35 mb/d in 1972. While 70 percent of the world's crude oil was refined at the source of 1939, by 1950 this share had decreased to 50 percent, and by 1973 it had declined to under 10 percent. This concentration of refineries near the growing West European markets led to the development of spot markets in oil products.

Beginning in the 1950s, trading in oil products quickly began to develop. Companies inexperienced in oil production but with backgrounds in shipping and coal became involved in the growing market for refined products and, especially, in the market for gas oil, a heating fuel. Although trade initially flowed down the Rhine River from the Federal Republic of Germany to the Low Countries, it soon expanded up-river, as independent refiners, particularly those in Italy, as well as the majors' refineries in Rotterdam, began to offer supplies to meet the growing German demand.[1] The market for gas oil, in particular, developed to supply the large German market. Rhine barges moved by canal into Bavaria, and into western Switzerland, as far as Basle. Much of this market was served by independent distributors without refineries of their own, who imported their products. It was as a result of the need to supply the German market, which traditionally was serviced by a large number of independent traders, that the first international spot market—for gas oil—developed.[2]

The spot trade in the Rotterdam market actually encompasses two separate types. One is barge trading, which covers the trade from the ARA ports (Antwerp/Rotterdam/Amsterdam) up the Rhine River to Germany, France, and Switzerland. The barge trade in products was first made possible by the concentration of refineries built by the majors in and near Rotterdam to serve inland markets, but was facilitated by the growing barge capacity and storage tanks built by such firms as Paktank to serve those markets. By the early 1960s, spot prices quoted for Rhine barge lots were becoming important worldwide as pricing indicators.

By the 1970s, spot quotes had expanded to include seagoing cargoes, as both consumers and producers increasingly dealt with supplies that were not subject to the majors' control. The trade in ocean cargoes is largely centered in London and covers international trade between ports around the world.

Today, products with prices linked to Rotterdam pricing come from a variety of places, but primarily from three sources: (1) the export refineries of the Mediterranean and, to some extent, those in the Caribbean; (2) the majors' refineries in the ARA area, France, and the United Kingdom (which has recently become an important source); and (3) the USSR and Eastern Europe. In addition, supplies have on occasion come from countries east of Suez, and more can be expected in the future from the refineries of the oil producing countries of the Arabian Gulf.

The buyers and sellers using the Rotterdam spot markets have changed over time. In the period from the mid-1960s to 1974, there was a large increase in the number of participants in the Rotterdam barge trade. Most of these new traders were independents. Prior to the assumption of control over pricing by the OPEC governments, the majors earned most of their profits on their upstream operations. In general, both product and crude prices were determined by the majors, and trade on the spot market had marginal impact on the price structure of the industry. The spot market was largely a *term market* and reflected the long-term, fixed-price contracts that characterized the industry as a whole. The major oil-firms were largely willing to let the independent traders manage the spot trade, and, while occasionally placing surplus lots of refined products on the market, they very rarely acted as spot buyers.

Although spot trading of crude also grew in the 1970s, the Rotterdam market has primarily been dominated by the trade in products. Owing to the capital-intensive nature of the refining industry, refiners have preferred to maintain access to a steady supply of crude through the use of long-term contracts, rather than rely on short-term spot purchases. Crude oil, therefore, has traditionally represented only a small portion of the Rotterdam trade.

Since the OPEC-induced industry upheaval of 1973–1974, however, the center of oil-industry profitability has shifted downstream. As a result, the larger oil firms have paid closer attention to the activities of the spot market. This became increasingly true as contract prices began to be linked, either directly or indirectly, to published spot prices. The existence of surplus refining capacity, as consumption dropped after the 1973–1974 price increases, and the growth of the spot market as a source of supply, have helped to end the tightly controlled long-term supply and price structure set by the large integrated oil-firms.

Although most of the world's oil products continue to be marketed through integrated channels and long-term contracts, increasing volumes of crude are moving through independent and national oil companies. As producers such as Kuwait—which sold up to 700,000 b/d on the spot market in 1980—have continued to make use of the Rotterdam market for crude, the majors have at times been driven to make spot crude-oil purchases to acquire refinery feedstocks to meet their commitments. The integrated oil firms now tend to buy more on the

Rotterdam market than they sell. The major refineries have thus reshaped their attitude toward the spot market, and some have established trading subsidiaries (for example, Shell's Petra, BP's Anco, and Exxon's Impco) in recognition of the new importance of the Rotterdam market. This new focus on the spot market means that most, but not all, of the major traders enjoy corporate backing.

The Mediterranean Spot Market

The growth of the Mediterranean spot market parallelled the postwar rise of the independent oil companies operating in Libya and Algeria, as refineries were built in Sicily and Sardinia to process North African crude oil. Italy, historically a major net importer of crude, took advantage of both its proximity to the Suez Canal and North Africa and the rising European demand for products by becoming a source of refined products for much of the rest of Europe.

Most of the crude processed by Mediterranean refineries was supplied from independents with no refineries of their own. The independents both supplied the crude and marketed the final products, minus the product that the refiners received as partial payment. Product was either trans-shipped to Trieste and sent by pipeline northwards to Bavaria, or was shipped by sea through Gibraltar to meet the demands of Northwest Europe (NWE). In particular, the Italian refineries were an important source of heavy fuel-oil. By the late 1960s, Italy had become a major source of product for the NWE area and, like Rotterdam at that time, a pricing center in its own right.

The refining capacity of the Mediterranean area was built to meet the burgeoning oil demand of the 1950s and 1960s. By the mid-1970s, however, as the world refinery industry slipped into a state of excess capacity, the Italian refineries proved to be marginal and suffered from a loss of markets. In addition, the interrupted use of the Suez Canal as a shipping route and the substitution of supertankers to carry crude around the Cape of Good Hope, reduced the geographical advantage of the Mediterranean industry. This advantage was further eroded as North Sea oil and natural gas began to replace Middle East and African imports.

For these reasons, the current Mediterranean market functions as a marginal source of supply. Owing to the Italian market's position as the shortest route from North Africa, Mediterranean (Med) spot prices are generally lower than those in Rotterdam. More than geography comes into play here, however; although Med prices would theoretically equal NWE prices less freight costs, they are usually slightly lower to be competitive.

The Mediterranean spot market operates in the shadow of the larger Rotterdam market. It functions less as a market in the traditional price-setting sense than it does as an important source of supply. Its convenient location near the major oil-producing centers of the Middle East and its huge capacity justify the

Table 6-1
Twenty Largest West European Refineries, 1981
(thousands of barrels per calendar day)

Country	Company	Location	Distillation Capacity
Austria	OMV	Schwechat	280
Belfium	Esso Belgium	Antwerp	250
	SIBP SA	Antwerp	366
Finland	Neste Oy	Porvoo	280
France	Cie Francaise de Raffinage	Gonfreville L'Orcher	500
	Shell Francaise	Petit-Couronne	382
Italy	Mediterranea SpA	Milazzo	505
	Raffineria del Po SpA	Sannazzaro Burgondi	230
	SARAS SpA	Sarroch (Caglian)	360
	SAROM Raffinazione SpA	Ravenna	250
	SARPOM	San Martino Di Trecata	257
Netherlands	BP Raffinaderij Nederland NV	Rotterdam	494
	Chevron Petroleum Mij (Nederland) NV	Pernis	260
	Shell Nederland Raffinaderij NV	Pernis	530
Portugal	Petroleas de Portugal	Sines	226
Spain	Petronor SA	Somorrostro (Vizcaya)	250
United Kingdom	BP Oil Kent Refinery	Isle of Grain	225
	ESSO Petroleum Company	Fawley	289
	Lindsey Oil Refinery	Killingholme	260
	Shell U.K.	Stanlow	250

Source: Adapted from *International Petroleum Times*, March 15, 1981, p. 31.

continued existence of the Mediterranean market to support the European spot trade in products. The importance of the Mediterranean market was highlighted in 1980 when the Italian refineries easily picked up the slack after Iran's huge Abadan refinery—the world's largest—was destroyed during the Iran-Iraq War.

Functions of the Rotterdam Market

The number of participants in the spot markets changes, and the variety of forces affecting them have been neither constant nor consistent. At all times, however, the market balances the supply and demand of individual countries, oil firms, refineries, and suppliers. Purchases and sales between these parties help each meet its needs, even though most transactions still take place through the integrated channels of the major oil-firms. Nevertheless, trade in the spot markets is designed:

1. to take product from or supply it to the integrated systems at the margins, when the main volumes have been balanced;
2. to take speculative positions, term and spot, and to buy for stock, speculating on seasonal price movements;
3. to mobilize supplies from outside the major integrated supply system; and
4. to act as a source for non-integrated downstream outlets.[3]

In performing these functions, the spot market operates only at the margin of supply and demand. The volume of the spot market, therefore, is relatively small compared to the total volume of products traded.

It is not certain what the actual size of the spot market is, precisely because the Rotterdam market is so amorphous and vaguely defined. The Commission of the European Communities (CEC) monitored both the Mediterranean and Northwest Europe markets in its Commission Market Analysis (COMMA), exercise conducted from June 1979 to May 1980, to determine more exactly the operations of these markets. The fifty-seven companies that participated reported their spot transactions weekly to the commission. The volume of valid transactions reported in this period was 43 million tonnes, of which 31 million tonnes were in the NWE European Economic Community (EEC minus Italy, plus Sweden and Switzerland) markets. The volume of unreported NWE spot trade was estimated at about 10 million tonnes, making total estimated NWE trade about 40 million tonnes. Net spot trade, that is, trade volume that does not include total trading activity and turnover but, only counts final trades, was estimated at 20 million tonnes. As measured against total inland deliveries of 410 million tonnes for that period, the COMMA report estimated that the spot market may account for approximately 5 percent of total inland trade. No estimate was made for the Mediterranean spot trade, about which less is known.

Spot trade volume, however, seems to have been lower than usual in the COMMA year. Estimates of the volume of net spot trade made in a 1978 exercise known as Checkrun were in the range of 30 million tonnes, suggesting that net spot trade could account for as much as 7–8 percent of total trade. The general assumption is that spot trade accounts for 5 percent–10 percent of total trade volume. The actual volume of spot trade fluctuates due to such factors as anticipated changes in demand availability of supply, the impact of seasonality, and changes in refining capacities. The most important factors affecting the level of activity in markets are the size of the independent sector and the extent to which demand is mismatched with refinery output.

Market Structure: Products

The Rotterdam market is dominated by the trade in gas oil and by the large German market. Gas oil is important because it accounts for about one-half of all trade and because of the many independents responsible for the distribution. Other products traded on the market, in order of relative importance, are heavy fuel-oil, naphtha, and motor gasolines (mogas). Trade in these products varies from year to year and is affected by three factors: (1) the structure of the down-stream market; (2) the technical properties of the product; and (3) the need for specialized handling and storage.[4]

Germany exerts a major influence on prices on the Rotterdam market. The Federal Republic is the largest independent market for oil products in Europe, counts on the spot market for much marginal supply, and has an energy-supply policy that relies upon the workings of the private sector to match supply with inland demand. The size of the German market means that it accounts for a large portion of the spot trade through the ARA ports and, thus, both strongly affects and is affected by Rotterdam prices. Although other national markets also are important—at times, for example, British purchases of premium motor gasoline led the market, and demand from Sweden has considerable impact on the low-sulphur fuel-oil market—none is as important as Germany.[5]

A breakdown of the product trade by volume, for the period covered by the COMMA study, showed that gas and fuel oil were the main products traded on the spot market, each accounting for about 38 percent of the total trade. Of the fuel-oil trade, high- and low-sulfur oil were traded at approximately a two-to-one ratio. Motor-gasoline trade was divided between premium and regular grades, with premium representing over 80 percent of the total trade in mogas. Examining the spot market in terms of barge and seagoing trade, the COMMA study indicated that gas oil dominated the barge trade with a 61 percent share, and that the 22 percent share held by fuel oil was divided nearly evenly between high- and low-sulfur oils. Naphtha constituted 7 percent of the barge trade. In contrast, trade in seagoing cargoes was composed of 41 percent fuel oil, with over half as high-sulfur fuel oil. Naphtha and gas oil each had a 25 percent share.

The differences in the product breakdown of the two types of trade can be attributed to the different parties involved in the barge and cargo markets. The barge trade is more concerned with gas oil for Rhine-fed heating-oil markets. Thus, the barge trade meets the needs of the independent traders active in sup-plying the German market. By way of contrast, the cargo market, which is an import market, reflects the involvement of refiners. The difference in market shares accounted for by naphtha in the barge trade and cargo trade (7 percent and 25 percent, respectively) dicates that in Europe naphtha is a net import product. Of naphtha spot sales covered by the COMMA study, cargo naphtha accounted for 68 percent of the total.[6]

Seasonality produces a somewhat predictable pattern on spot-market prices and volumes. In general, trade in the summer months reflects increased consumption of mogas, while winter trade is dominated by heating oil. Since spot trade is marginal, however, it may vary from the regular pattern of trade. Thus, as shown by the COMMA report, seasonality may affect spot markets differently than it does regular-market activity.

Market Structure: Prices

The soaring of spot prices above contract prices and the volatility of the market in 1979 shows the spot trade operating at the margin of supply and demand. The spot markets in crude and products registered sharp increases in both volume and price in response to the tight market conditions caused by some cuts in production, increased stockpiling, and supply uncertainty in the aftermath of the Iranian Revolution. The turbulence that characterized world spot markets in this period focused attention on Rotterdam and raised questions in the minds of European consumers and their governments about the role of the spot trade in the petroleum industry.

In times of crude-oil capacity surplus, which represents the normal state of affairs, spot prices tend to be in line with, or slightly less than, prices in long-term contracts. This was true for the period from 1975 through the end of 1978. The scramble for oil supplies in the tight market in 1979, however, reversed this pricing relationship. Conditions of real or perceived shortages force spot-product prices above contract prices. The 1979–1980 collapse of the Iranian oil industry, exacerbated by the war with Iraq and the accompanying destruction of oil facilities, is but the most recent example of a condition that causes supply uncertainty.

In this period, not only were spot product and crude markets disrupted, but the spot market, in turn, placed upward pressure on the contract market. As producer governments watched spot-crude prices climb in 1979, they demanded, and received, premiums linked to spot prices on the oil sold under long-term contracts. Oil exporters took this opportunity both to diversify their sales away from the majors and to increase government revenues. For an estimated 10 mb/d of contract crude, price premiums levied by exporting countries were based upon spot-market prices. The link between spot and contract prices in 1979 sparked consumer complaints that the tail was wagging the dog; that is, spot prices, although based on transactions that occur at the margins of the world petroleum market, were leading regular-market prices.

When fears concerning the supply of crude oil eased in 1980, spot-crude volumes shrank and prices fell to near official posted levels. In the first three months of 1980, an estimated 700,000 b/d of crude was traded in spot sales, well below the record 3 mb/d traded in the last nine months of 1979.

The pendulum continued to swing in early 1981 as a Saudi-engineered oil glut appeared. During the period of supply surpluses in the first part of 1981, for example, spot-market crude-oil prices began to slip below official sales prices. By June 1981, even Saudi marker crude was trading at prices lower than the official prices.

Price Information Sources

Despite the importance of spot-market prices, however, there is no formal price-reporting mechanism. By the nature of a spot market, prices can vary with each transaction. Nevertheless, there are several means by which representative prices are reported. The most authoritative is the daily report compiled by *Platt's Oilgram Price Service,* published in the United States. The price assessments listed by Platts are exactly that: compiled after telephone calls with traders in the market, they take into account not only sale prices, but also bids and offers, and assessments are published even for days when no actual sales take place. As a result, Platt's prices do not necessarily cover the actual highs or lows of trading prices, nor do they really show average prices.

As an assessment of prices, Platt's tends to lag behind the market. This is true both when prices and volumes are moving rapidly and when trade is slow, as it is in the spring and summer, when oil demand drops and the Rhine may be too low to permit barge movement. Despite this, however, Platt's prices are widely regarded as a reasonably reliable indicator of the market. Platts prices are referred to by both private and government groups. Some EEC governments use Platt's assessments as a basis for the border pricing of products for tax collection purposes.

The New York-based *Petroleum Intelligence Weekly* provides high-quality bits of insider news and is another important source of price and other industry-related information. Other guides to Rotterdam prices include *The Petroleum Argus,* published twice weekly in the United Kingdom, and the U.S. weekly *Oil Buyers Guide.*

None of these publications present a precise account of actual prices. Instead, they give an impression of price levels and general indices of trends. To date, there is no permanent, formal statistical price-reporting system.

In recognition of the impact of the spot market on petroleum markets, the CEC established a Bourse Study Group to examine the feasibility of a formal bourse for oil products. In a 1980 communication, the Commission observed that there is no official information on prices or volumes of trade in the Rotterdam market, despite the common reliance on spot quotes as a basis for long-term deals, inter-affiliate transfer prices, and consumer price formulae.

Although the Commission did not feel that either a bourse or a permanent price-reporting system such as that adopted for the COMMA study would be warranted, it did recommend a greater transparency in Rotterdam prices. To this end, the CEC noted the possible value of the initiatives then taken by the

London Commodity Exchange to establish a futures market in oil products, the International Petroleum Exchange. In particular, they felt that such an exchange would be useful both in providing a supplemental price-reporting system systematically linked to prices on the spot market and in helping to smooth price fluctuations.

Notes

1. Joe Roeber, *The Rotterdam Oil Market* (London: Petroleum Economist, Petroleum Press Bureau Ltd., April 1979), p. 2.
2. Inter Commodities Limited, "The Gas Oil Report" (London: March, 1981), p. 6.
3. Roeber, "The Rotterdam Oil Market," p. 3.
4. Ibid., p. 3.
5. Ibid., p. 5.
6. Joe Roeber Associates, "COMMA: The EEC Register of Spot Transactions—Summary and Conclusions of the Final Report," (Brussels: Directorate-General for Energy, Commission of the European Communities, 22 October, 1980), p. 3.

7 A Typical London Oil-Trading Office

Kenneth Potter

Trading Offices

In London, the brokers and traders associated with the insurance, finance, and shipping businesses are nearly all to be found congregated in the city. Most oil-trading offices are in or near the center of the West End, where the head offices of most of the major oil-companies also are situated.

The average trading offices, consisting of a few rooms in a well-appointed building, are small centers of concentrated activity where members of a highly skilled staff make important decisions and exercise mature judgment.

The chief executive may be the managing director of the United Kingdom unit of an international trading company, the major shareholder of a partnership, or sometimes the sole proprietor of a trading firm. Whichever role he fills, he is most likely to be the full-time chief executive and is expected to be in charge twenty-four hours a day. As a back-up team, he will have two or three assistants and one or two secretary/bookkeepers. A total staff of six can have an annual turnover of $500 million.

To achieve this volume of trade it is essential that they work as a team, each aware of what the others currently have inhand and able to take over at a moments notice. Fast communication is the essence of successful trading; for this reason, the telex machine is a vital part of the office equipment.

Because traders and brokers have clients around the world, time differences between countries, as well as the continuous movement of ships and operation of oil fields, requires that someone will be available all during the day to make decisions and take action. When the office is closed, at least one member of the trading firm will usually be available at their home telephone. It is an exacting business, where important decisions may need to be made at all hours of the day and night throughout the year.

The Difference between Traders and Brokers

Oil brokers and traders are integral and important parts of the energy industry. Despite popular confusion concerning their separate functions, one can differentiate. The oil broker is a middleman who will arrange a purchase and sale between two parties, for a commission, on terms acceptable to both. Providing he has a succession of business, his financial exposure and risk is minimal compared to that of a trader. The oil trader, on the other hand, is a principal who buys from a supplier under one set of conditions, and sells to a purchaser on different terms. The trader's profits hinge on negotiating terms that yield a margin between his acquisition costs and selling price. Obviously, his financial exposure is high in the initial cost of a cargo or series of cargoes. Equally, his risk can be high, particularly in times of changing market conditions.

Cargo sizes vary, but in general terms crude cargoes are usually between 70,000 and 250,000 tonnes, and product cargoes are about 30,000 tonnes. With values in the order of $230 and $300–$400 per tonne, respectively, it is apparent that a trader needs to have very sound credit backing. The volatility to which petroleum markets have often been subject means that any firm procuring product or crude cargoes in expectation of making a profit on the margins is exposed to great risks.

In Europe, the second largest port in the world—Rotterdam—is the center of maritime oil movements. In spite of this, however, London has become the center of most of the oil-trading business in Western Europe. While some trading companies retain offices in their home countries, notably in Hamburg, the Hague, Rotterdam, Brussels, Antwerp, and Paris, many of them have moved their main center to London in recent years.

Although there are always some changes taking place in the pattern of newcomers to and those moving away from the oil-trading business, the total number of operators remains relatively small and fairly static. In London, there are probably less than fifty traders and about a dozen brokers. The larger number of traders probably reflects their general acceptance as members of the petroleum industry, playing a permanent role in the route from oilfield to end users.

It is usual for both brokers and traders to confine their activities to dealing either in crude oil or finished refined products, seldom mixing the two types of business. The primary reason for this segregation is that, while the basic principles of the crude and products markets are similar, conditions affecting crude and product trading vary considerably. There is some spot dealing in crude, but, in general, most crude-oil deals involve contractual time spans to ensure the continuous operation of a refinery and the continuous off-take of crude from the oilfield. This situation prevails despite the apparent increase in crude offered for spot purchase that has occurred in recent years. The crude-oil trader, moreover, will also be able to provide flexibility to refiners by exchanges of specific types of crude to satisfy specific refinery patterns. This flexibility is not characteristic of the trade in products. These different considerations, as well as the experience and interests of the traders themselves, make it a usual practice for a firm to specialize in one field or the other.

The Roles and Skills of Brokers and Traders

The oil industry already is over-populated with producers, refiners, and distributors to serve the industry and the public. The reason for traders and brokers lies in a complex combination of supply, demand, storage, shipping, and logistics. Traders and brokers are experts in these areas and frequently are able to provide flexibility to the industry in a way that cannot be achieved as effectively by any one oil producing, refining, or marketing unit, however large it may be. The broker and particularly the trader have been able to help the world petroleum industry in smoothing out high and low spots and maintaining regional, national, and company balances between supply and demand.

To effectively juggle supplies and maintain a smooth distribution flow, traders must be skilled in many different disciplines. Of course, the most basic need is adequate technical knowledge of petroleum to identify and negotiate the specification criteria required and offered by buyer and seller. Traders, moreover, must be sufficiently well-versed in the operations of the world petroleum industry and financial markets to:

arrange the required credit to span the time between the seller's physically parting with his products and his receiving payment for them;

keep themselves informed of the international supply-and-demand position and the current limits of price fluctuations on a day-to-day basis (they must know where to buy and sell, who is long, who is short, and for what reasons); and

stay familiar with all the detailed terms and conditions of ship chartering.

Naturally, traders must be good negotiators and be sufficiently bold (and wise) to take acceptable commercial risks. Above all, one cannot become a good oil trader without first earning an international reputation for high integrity and impeccable ethical dealing.

Looking at these skills and qualities, it is reasonable to seek the background of such men. In general, they begin as junior members of a trading office, bringing with them command of one or more of the necessary skills. They may have previously worked for oil companies, banks, ship charterers, shipping companies, other traders or brokers, but usually they arrive with a built-in flair for negotiation.

Newcomers must rapidly acquire knowledge and experience in new areas, and, thereafter, their professional progress will depend upon their performance and the reputations they earn. At the present time, in all of Europe, there probably are not more than ten top-rate traders. Traders stand or fall by their integrity and they guard their reputations with jealous zeal. The salaries of members to this select club are commensurate with their caliber and the demands made upon them.

Trading

Most product traders do not indulge in highly speculative situations by buying forward in anticipation of shortage, unusually cold weather, political unrest, or other extremes. Instead they provide themselves with a sensible minimum availability by forward purchase, crude-oil processing, or options, and then develop business on a supply/demand or back-to-back basis. In other words, traders strive to arrange both the purchase and resale at the same time, thereby reducing their financial risks to a minimum.

Such deals frequently originate with refiners who, during certain times of the year, find that they have a surplus of particular product beyond their downstream marketing needs. This can occur, for example, in summer when a refinery is producing a maximum gasoline yield. Under these conditions, the refinery could develop gas oil in excess of its summer marketing needs. The trader who knows of this situation can search the market for a buyer. If successful, he will buy product from the refiner and try coincidentally to make a back-to-back sale.

This sounds like a simple operation; in fact, many complex procedures and formalities are necessary to success. First, the refiner will wish to have a guarantee that payment will be made against delivery. The trader, as principal, will already have needed to establish a banking credit to satisfy this requirement. In addition, if he is taking the product by sea as an FOB purchase, he will need to charter a ship to transport it to his buyer's destination, if his sale is made on a CIF basis (cost insurance freight). On the other hand, the trader must specify similar criteria to protect himself in his dealings with the refiner, and at the same time satisfy the requirements of his buyer. For example, the trader will require guarantees as to the quality of the oil products, and the timeliness of delivery.

There will be letters of credit to arrange, the ship to be charter, insurance cover to make. Independent inspection of quality at both ports of loading and discharge must be arranged and paid for by one party or the order. The time allowed for loading and discharge (lay time), and the rates of demurrage if these times are exceeded, are just some of the matters that have to be decided and properly recorded before each deal is concluded.

If one considers that the three parties involved—the seller, the trader, and the final buyer—might be located on three different continents, the need for clear definitions, decisive action, and fast communication is obvious. Reviewing the many areas of detailed variance that can occur in a deal involving just one cargo will emphasize how much the knowledge, the standing, and the reputation of an oil trader will influence the success of his business. It is for this reason that, once established, good reputations are maintained with great care.

A top-ranking product trader will try to handle an average of about four cargoes per month, each of about 30,000 tonnes. This means an annual turnover of some $500 million, upon which his losses could be $5 million if all deals go the wrong way (a $3 per tonnes loss) or $2.5 million gross profit if all the deals go the right way. From this figure, of course, considerable costs and expenses have to be deducted before the true profit picture is seen. In practice, like every other kind of trading, the end result is usually somewhere between these two extremes. It must also be remembered that achieving a successful cargo sale once a week throughout the year requires a great deal of effort and, occasionally, a little bit of luck.

**Part III
Oil-Futures Markets**

8 Why Are There Futures Markets?

Oil-Futures Markets

Futures trading for petroleum products developed for the classic reason that led to futures trading in other commodities: there was not enough price stability. The once predictable international oil market has suffered severe bouts of price volatility. Oil has been increasingly used for political ends since at least 1970, as was well highlighted by the Arab oil exporters' embargo in 1973-1974. The absence of an open price-determination process, the seasonality of demand for many petroleum products (particularly gas oil and gasoline), the presence of a large number of buyers and sellers for these products, and the importance of oil to the industrialized world make oil a commodity for which futures trading is not only appropriate, but extremely necessary.

Attempts to set a trade in petroleum futures contracts date from 1971, with the introduction of a propane contract by the newly-formed Petroleum Associates of the New York Cotton Exchange. While trade in this contract was initially slow, it increased significantly during the period of December 1973 through January 1974, reflecting the reaction to the Arab oil embargo, which had begun in October 1973.

In 1974, futures contracts in gas oil were introduced in Amsterdam and in New York. The Amsterdam contracts, for one hundred tonnes, was for Rotterdam delivery. This contract, which began trading on September 6, 1974, was initiated by the Forward Contract Exchange Company (U.K.), which began operations in Amsterdam in 1973 by offering futures contracts in stock-exchange indices.

On September 10, 1974, the Petroleum Associates of the New York Cotton Exchange introduced a crude-oil futures contract for Rotterdam delivery. The standard contract was for 5,000 barrels of $34°$ *American Petroleum Institute* (API), 1.7 percent sulfur-content crude, the specifications of Saudi Arabian light crude. Other crudes of between $27°$ to $45°$ API gravity, and of between 0.1 percent to 3.0 percent sulfur, were deliverable at a discount or at a premium.

Also in 1974, the New York Mercantile Exchange introduced futures contracts, for Rotterdam delivery, for No. 2 oil (gas oil) and for No. 6 oil (residual fuel oil). The introduction of oil contracts in 1974 on three exchanges reflected the concern sparked by the 1973-1974 embargo and the sudden turmoil reverberating on world petroleum markets.

This concern, however, was not sufficiently widespread among industry members to sustain all of these contracts, and trading in each of them collapsed fairly soon after their introduction. This is attributable to two major factors. First, trading in petroleum futures was initiated by persons involved in the futures-trading industry and not by those within the oil industry. Introduction of the contracts immediately after the effects of the oil embargo was premature. Too few participants in the petroleum industry understood the dynamics of futures trading or recognized the benefits of oil futures. Futures traders, on the other hand, were insufficiently versed in the particulars of the oil industry.

While to a financial mind futures trading in oil involves the same concepts as futures trading in other commodities, the oil industry tended to view it as untried and unfamiliar. Maybe it still does. Many individuals unfamiliar with futures trading were under the impression that futures markets compete with traditional long-term merchandising contracts. This is not the case. Futures contracts do not replace long-term agreements, but exist in tandem with them as a financial mechanism to coordinate transactions and diminish the effects of price changes. Futures trading also provides a market of last resort for the procurement of marginal supplies.

Second, the imposition in 1971 of price controls on petroleum and petroleum products in the United States had made price behavior fairly predictable. Futures trading in U.S. domestic circles was curtailed. Only those traders with international ties were interested in these new futures contracts. While prices in Europe were not regulated as in the U.S., after the effects of the price increases were absorbed, many analysts expected price levels to remain stable. The prices of European product, moreover, have historically been considerably higher than those in the United States because of the higher petroleum-products taxes levied by the European countries. This partially blunted the effect on end-users in Western Europe, where price increases stemming from the jump in crude prices were a little bit less dramatic than they were in the United States.

U.S. Price Controls

In August 1971, President Nixon imposed general price-controls on many segments of the economy. Oil was no exception. Oil companies were required to sell their products to the public within fixed price ranges. This eliminated the free market conditions necessary for a futures market. Price controls meant minimum price volatility and ended the need for propane futures, which had been introduced in July 1971. The imposition of the Nixon administration's phase I price controls pushed back the development of U.S. petroleum futures-trading for domestic delivery.

In 1974, NYMEX introduced contracts for No. 2 heating oil and for No. 4 heavy oil for delivery in Rotterdam. While Rotterdam delivery enabled handlers to trade gas oil unencumbered by U.S. price restrictions, the foreign delivery-point rendered the 1974 contract less interesting to the North American market. Although only a very small percentage of futures contract are settled by actual physical delivery of product, delivery must be feasible for the contract to have any meaning. The additional expense and inconvenience of moving a gas-oil cargo from Rotterdam to the United States diminished the possible advantages of the contract.

In 1975, Congress passed and President Ford signed the Energy Policy and Conservation Act, placing limits on the annual increase in the price of most domestic crude-oils. The law also allowed for this provision to be phased out with an end to all price controls on petroleum products in 1981.

Gas oil was exempted from price controls in four out of five states in 1976 because adequate supplies were available again. This set the stage for a futures market in No. 2: there was sufficient price freedom to make futures trading attractive, a lot of people were interested, trading volume looked to be sizeable, and maybe the timing was right.

The New York Mercantile Exchange kicked-off trading futures-contracts for No. 2 heating oil and for No. 6 heavy fuel-oil, for delivery in the New York Harbor area, on November 14, 1978. The No. 6 contract has been inactive, due primarily to the relatively small number of potential users, most of whom chose long-term contracts for their supply. The electric utilities, which used approximately 380 million barrels of No. 6 in 1980, are answerable to state public-utility commissions for the cost of electricity and prefer not to hedge on residual fuel-oil purchases. Explaining to the public that the price of fuel has increased, and that rates must therefore increase, is a difficult enough public-relations task for the utilities. Having to explain that an error in futures-trading judgment has resulted in higher electric rates is unthinkable for utility managements. On both sides of the Atlantic, production and consumption of No. 6 oil is declining. On top of all this, residual oils are low-profit products, often being sold at or even below costs. This reduces their desirability to refiners, as well as to participants in futures trading.

The No. 2 NYMEX contract, which will be discussed in depth in chapter 10, has been a popular one, and, after only three years, is the most actively traded contract on the New York Merc. Previous to the establishment of this trading, it was assumed by many that oil prices could only rise. Partial decontrol, however, proved that this was not the case, and that short selling could be a useful tool for producers and consumers alike.

Price Deregulation

The complete deregulation of domestic-oil prices by President Reagan in February 1981 accelerated the decontrol that had been scheduled to be completed by

October of that year. A heavy weight had been lifted at last from the shoulders of would-be oil-futures traders. Although attempts had been made previously to establish trading in petroleum futures, the concept was not at all well established in 1978, when NYMEX opened trading in gas oil. Another major contributor to the growth in trading gas-oil futures has been the efforts made by NYMEX to educate the business world and general public about the usefulness of a futures market in these oil products.

Even so, the contract got off to a slow start. Despite its rapid growth over the last few years, many oil industry people remain skeptical about the need of the oil-futures trade. The volume of gas oil traded on NYMEX, moreover, is an insignificant fraction of the national and even regional turnover. This is very important. A tiny chunk of the oil trade, as measured by the futures markets turnover, looms large in contrast to the futures trading in, for example, an agricultural commodity, or nickel on the London Metal Exchange (LME), but is still relatively insignificant to the world oil industry. This means, of course, that the oil-futures market may not now or ever achieve the status of such a trade as the copper trade on the LME as a pricing indicator for the world industry.

NYMEX's efforts have been mentioned to illustrate a crucial point: the handlers of a commodity must be active trading participants for a futures market in that product to survive. Heating-oil futures provide the same speculative opportunities, in principle, as do other commodity contracts. A great deal of the trade by *locals*—the floor traders of a particular exchange—is carried out by individuals lacking any technical knowledge of petroleum. The locals are familiar, however, with the price behavior of, as well as the fundamentals of trading futures in, that product, and their speculative trade provides vital liquidity to the market. Speculation is not, however, sufficient to sustain a market. The education effort by NYMEX was necessary to ensure the participation of gas-oil handlers, without whom the contract would have failed.

Meanwhile, a somewhat similar set of commercial forces were at work in Western Europe. The traditional antipathy of major oil firms to futures trading was true also in Europe, and there were fewer small oil firms to provide material for a possible futures-market. The structure of the European oil market is not totally different from that of the United States, and it was logical that an oil-futures market could be developed in time. Pushed along by the upheavals of the 1978–1979 Iranian Revolution and the subsequent Iranian-Iraqi border war, the International Petroleum Exchange began trading in London on April 6, 1981. The IPE contract is for one hundred tonnes of gas oil, with delivery in the ARA port areas.

In August 1981, NYMEX added a No. 2 contract specifying United States Gulf Coast delivery (specified ports in Louisiana, Mississippi, and Texas). The Chicago Board of Trade also applied to the Commodity Futures Trading Commission (CFTC) for designation as a contract market for trading in No. 2 futures for Gulf Coast delivery. The CFTC approved a spate of oil-futures contracts in the fall of 1981. The proposal and approval of NYMEX regular leaded and unleaded gasoline futures for delivery in the New York Harbor area and similar contracts for Gulf Coast delivery may presage a growth in the U.S. futures trade in terms of products and geographic diversity. Before the close of the year, the CBT received approval for its Louisiana crude-oil contract for Gulf Coast delivery. The New York Cotton Exchange, lastly, initiated a new liquified propane gas contract in December 1981, rescusitating its earlier failed effort. Whether or not any of these contracts can stay the course and attract real interest from traders is very uncertain at this early stage.

9

The Gas-Oil
Futures Market

Refining

Before discussing gas-oil futures, we will describe how gas oil is made and what it is. Like all oil products, gas oil starts out as crude oil. Crude oil typically consists of a mixture of paraffinic hydrocarbons, ranging from gases to asphaltic, tarry compounds. The fundamental property that distinguishes one petroleum fraction from another is its specific gravity, which is chiefly dependent upon the length of the straight-chain hydrocarbon, or more simply, the number of carbon atoms in the molecule. These different components in a barrel of crude petroleum are separated by refining. At its most basic, this is a process of boiling and differential condensations.

The first step in refining is to separate the crude oil into its basic fractions by the relatively simple process of *straight run* distillation. In this step, the crude is vaporized by heating and passed into a fractioning tower, where the vapors rise through a series of trays and cool. The temperatures are highest at the bottom of the tower and lowest at the top. As the vapors rise, various cuts or fractions condense into liquids at each level, depending upon their condensation point. The heaviest material (having the highest boiling point) condenses and stays at the bottom of the tower, and the lightest material (having the lowest boiling point) condenses at the top. The liquids, as they condense, are captured in the trays at the different levels of the fractioning tower and from there are piped away.

The crude-oil components segregated by the straight run include the lighter gasoline, naptha, and kerosene fractions; the middle distillates, which is the group to which gas oil belongs; and the residual distillates, including heavy fuel-oil. The product mix ensuing from straight-run refining depends upon the crude being distilled. A heavy crude oil, with a specific gravity of .86 or higher, for example, will produce a higher percentage of residual fuels than will a light crude with a lower specific gravity of .80.[1]

Through additional and more complex procedures, such as thermal cracking, catalytic cracking, or hydrocracking, the straight-run products are further separated and refined. Thermal cracking involves very high temperatures and pressures to breakdown heavy fuel-oils. Catalytic cracking is a chemical procedure that causes the straight-run products to break down into lighter products, including gasoline, without using high temperatures and pressures. In hydrocracking, the addition of hydrogen reshapes the molecules and increases the yield of certain products. The amount of each product per barrel at any one refinery is determined by the refining processes utilized at that particular plant. In general, gas oil, after it is separated through distillation, is not subjected to any further refining processes, except desulfurization to reduce the sulfur content to acceptable levels.

Gas Oil

Gas oil is a middle-distillate petroleum fraction with a specific-gravity range of approximately .81 to .92. Most commercial gas oil is sold at a specific gravity of about .84. Commercial gas oil is primarily used as home-heating fuel and as fuel for diesel engines.

Gas oil has many different names in different countries, but the products are essentially the same. In the United States, gas oil is sold as No. 2 heating oil for use in space heating, and also as diesel oil for vehicles. In the United Kingdom, it is known as gas oil for heating or as Derv fuel, for diesel-engine road vehicles. In the Federal Republic of Germany, Derv reappears as diesel (in honor of the German designer of that engine), and the heating fuel is called ELHO (for extra light heating oil). The use of the term "gas oil" arose at the beginning of the twentieth century, when the product was added to enrich the content of British thermal units (Btu) in town gas, a fuel product made from coal. Today, town gas is upgraded by the addition of natural gas.

Gas oil has a variety of end uses. It is most commonly employed as a fuel for industrial, commercial, and residential space-heating. It finds applications as a process control fuel, although the temperature regulation is not as precise as that for natural gas. Gas oil also is used in the electric-utility industry, in industrial steam production, as a feedstock in the petrochemical industry, as a fuel for internal-combustion diesel engines, and, through cracking, as a feedstock in the production of high-grade gasolines.

The major distinction between the different grades of gas oil used for these various purposes is their specific gravity. Gas oil with a specific gravity of .81 would be considered too light and substandard, gas oil with a specific gravity of .82 would be considered normal; and gas oil with a specific gravity of .84 would be prime quality heating-oil. Gas oil with a higher specific gravity will burn with a higher caloric content, generating more heat. Lighter oils are more appropriate for burning in high compression internal-combustion engines. Gas oil used for heating can be of a heavier grade.

Refining and Specifications

Since 1950, the upgrading of refinery processes to produce gasoline with higher octane levels has also yielded higher quality heating oil.[2] Increased environmental concerns in the United States and Western Europe have prompted a general reduction in the sulfur content of gas oil. The maximum percentage of sulfur allowed varies from one country to another. Gas oil is usually sold containing the maximum permissible sulfur content because of the prohibitive cost of the additional desulfurization processes.

In the Federal Republic of Germany (FRG), Belgium, the Netherlands, and Sweden, for instance, the maximum amount of sulfur allowed is 0.3 percent by weight, whereas in Switzerland it is 0.5 percent. In Greece, Turkey, and the Far East, the requirements are even less stringent.

No. 2 heating oil sold on NYMEX must conform to New York City environmental regulations, which are among the most strict in the United States. The NYMEX contract sets a sulfur limit of 0.2 percent by weight. Gas oil traded on the International Petroleum Exchange in London, however, has a maximum allowable sulfur content of 0.3 percent by weight.

Refining also allows an adjustment of the wax content of the fuel (measured by the *cloud point*) in accordance with seasonal conditions. Gas oil used during winter or in colder climates must have a lower wax content than that used in the summer or in warmer areas, as cold temperatures can cause the wax to crystallize and seize-up any piping. Acceptable wax content, therefore, is lower in winter than in summer. And, the colder the geographic area, the lower the level of acceptable wax content. For example, the wax content for Sweden is below that for the rest of Europe.

The specific gravity, sulfur content, and cloud point of gas oil all affect its quality, and accordingly, its price. Of these three, specific gravity is the most important quality factor, followed by sulfur content. Although product of inferior quality can be traded at a discount, gas oil physically delivered in settlement of an IPE or NYMEX futures contract must meet the minimum contract specifications.

Supply and Demand

Gas oil is the largest fraction of the middle distillates produced during the refining process. Actual refinery yields per barrel of crude vary according to the type of crude processed, the design of the refinery, and the requirements of demand. Middle distillate fuels accounted for 28 percent of the total volume of product yield from North American refineries in recent years. For Western Europe and Japan, middle distillates account for 36 percent and 30 percent of refined product, respectively.

The demand for gas oil, since it is used primarily as a heating fuel, is strongly affected by the time of year. Inventories are built up annually from late spring through early fall in preparation for winter. These inventories are depleted by the time spring arrives and the cycle is begun again. Consumption of gas oil depends upon the severity of the winter. This traditional relationship may have become less predictable in recent years, as high prices have led to increased conservation. In Western Europe, the widespread conversion to natural gas in home-heating systems has also shaved peak winter demand for gas oil.

In the United States, for example, one of the first indications that this relationship may have been eroding occured in December 1980, when heating-oil consumption on the East Coast was lower than during the previous December, although the prior year had been much warmer. While the correlation between the level of consumption and the severity of the winter may be lessening, it still exists, and the seasonal build-up and draw-down of inventories—which makes futures trading in gas oil a valuable option to producers and consumers—remains the same.

The supply of gas oil, which is predicated to a large extent upon the changes of season, is also tied to the demand for, and the supply of, motor gasoline. Automobile fuel is the most important petroleum product in terms of volume and value, and the refinery output of gas oil can be inversely related to the production of gasoline. When demand for gasoline is high, middle distillates will often be used as a feedstock to increase the volume of gasoline produced, and the production of gas oil will decline. Typically, the production of gasoline is greater in the late winter, spring and early summer, in response to the increased consumption of motor fuel during the warmer months. The percentage of gas oil produced, on the other hand, is greater in the late summer, fall, and early winter. As refiner profits are largely determined by gasoline sales, the supply of gas oil beyond minimal stock needs is usually a consequence of making more gasoline, rather than of the demand for gas oil.

In the long term, the increasing use of diesel-powered vehicles in the United States may lead to increased demand for diesel transport fuel and, therefore, for gas oil. Various forecasts estimate that automotive diesel fuel demand will even double during the balance of this century. Thus, owners of fleets of diesel-powered cars and trucks, as well as the producers and dealers of diesel fuel, are potential participants in futures markets. Today, diesel-powered vehicles remain a distinct minority of cars and trucks produced.

Potential Markets for Gas-Oil Futures

There are various groups to whom futures trading in No. 2 oil could be advantageous.

Distributors. In most industrialized countries, gas oil is a key fuel for home heating, and it is subject to the price changes inherent in the seasonality of its use. The high demand for No. 2 during the autumn and winter months also requires that distributors build large inventories during spring and summer. Because of the relatively short selling season, distributors are aware of being vulnerable to shortages and short-term price increases. Futures contracts, through their use as a price-pegging tool, can greatly minimize the exposure of these distributors to vagaries in the price and supply of No. 2 oil.

Refiners. Long-term contracts for the delivery of refined products—such as No. 2—generally no longer specify a fixed price for product. They are primarily commitments whereby the seller is assured of a purchaser, and the buyer knows there is a source of supply. The refiner is, thus, vulnerable to losses in the event that the price of No. 2 were to decline during the time between his purchase of crude and his eventual sale of refined product. This can definitely happen with a product such as gas oil, owing to the seasonality of demand.

Through hedging, the refiner can try to offset losses which he might otherwise suffer from falling prices. While hedging may limit the potential profits in a favorable market, it lets the refiner fix his operating margin to a high degree, enabling him to operate his business more efficiently.

Jobbers. Jobbers fulfill the wholesaler function by purchasing product from refiners and selling it to large commercial consumers, as well as to distributors (who in turn retail it to their customers). Jobbers can benefit from the futures market in much the same way as distributors and refiners: they can limit potential losses from a downswing in prices, they can profit by hedging against inventories, and they can increase the efficiency of their businesses by fixing profit margins.

Industrial and Commercial Consumers. Consumers of very large quantities of No. 2 fuel, either as a raw material (for the petrochemical industry, for instance) or as a boiler fuel, can benefit by taking advantage of the futures markets. Organizations that require large amounts of gas oil for their operations need to be assured of supplies at a relatively stable price. Hedging allows the actual net cost incurred to be fixed in advance.

Companies that require large amounts of gas oil as a transportation fuel or as a heating fuel also can benefit from the price-fixing function of a futures market. Automobile rental companies, bus fleets, trucking concerns, office buildings, and residential complexes are typical of the groups that can limit their financial exposure by hedging.

It is important to recall that hedging can be effective between different but similar products. The most important element of hedging is parallel price movement. Theoretically, hedging in gas oil can be undertaken by assuming a futures position in any product whose price behavior is parallel to that of gas oil. Were there to be, for some reason, a strict correlation between the price of gas oil and the price of bananas, hedging could be successfully executed between the two. In this way, a futures market in No. 2 oil can be used by consumers of other petroleum products, as the price trends of many petroleum products are approximately parallel. The price parallels between No. 2 oil and naphtha, for example, permits users of naphtha (for which there is no futures contract) to hedge costs against futures in No. 2.

The possibility of a settlement by delivery generally makes hedging between dissimilar products unwise. It is hard to burn bananas instead of gas oil, no matter what premium is offered! One can utilize a futures position in heating oil, however, to moderate the effect of spot-market price changes in jet fuel or in gasoline, for example.

Notes

1. Specific gravity is the ratio of the density of oil to the density of water. This should not be confused with API (American Petroleum Institute) gravity, which is measured in degrees. API gravity is the standard industry system of grading crude oil and is expressed by the formula $°API = 141.5/SG \ 60/65°F. - 131.5$, which gives water an API gravity of 10.

The specific gravity ranges of several petroleum products are included in chapter 8.

2. The specifications of the products deliverable by the various petroleum-futures contracts are contained in the contracts, which are appendixes E-I.

10 New York Mercantile Exchange

New York Harbor No. 2-Oil Contract

The New York Mercantile Exchange began trading No. 2 heating-oil contracts for New York Harbor delivery in 1978. In the course of just over three years, the No. 2 contract has become the exchange's most actively traded futures contract and currently is the most rapidly growing futures commodity in the United States. A daily average of more than 5,000 contracts in No. 2 oil were traded during 1981.

Trading volume for 1981 was some 600 percent greater than the total volume of 115,000 contracts traded in 1980. October 1981 trading alone saw more contracts change hands than in all of the previous year. The total 1979 volume, by comparison, was less than 12,000 trades. This was only slightly more than one-third of the turnover during May 1981, the slowest month of the year (when 33,000 contracts were traded), and less than the 12,456 contracts traded on October 22, 1981, a record-breaking day.

Open interest—the number of unmatured contracts outstanding—on October 1, 1981, stood at 37,000 contracts, accounting for roughly 37 million barrels of No. 2 oil. Open interest has increased steadily since the introduction of the contract in 1978, continually setting records.

The participation of hedgers is attested to by the number of deliveries expressed as a percentage of the total volume of contracts traded. This is a very significant figure because of the importance of hedging to the survival of trade in a futures contract. During 1981, deliveries averaged just under 2 percent of contracts traded, down significantly from an average of 4 percent during 1980, and from the erratic figures of 1979. (Deliveries in October 1979, admittedly a freak month, accounted for over two-thirds of contracts traded!) Table 10-1 shows the volume of trade and frequency of deliveries for 1980 and 1981.

The viability of the No. 2 New York contract is attested to by the steady growth in the volume of its trade. Confidence in the market is reflected in the marked decline in the frequency of actual deliveries in 1981, which is evidence of the contracts usefulness as a financial or hedging tool. During 1981, the settling price for No. 2 contracts was within the range of New York spot prices (as reported by Platt's) eight out of twelve times. For the remaining four months, the price was off by less than one half cent per gallon. The high degree of cash convergence for the New York contract justifies the reliance placed in it by hedgers. Table 10-2 contrasts the quarterly price of New York nearbys and spot prices for heating oil, as well as the national average.

Table 10-1
New York Harbor, No. 2 Heating-Oil Contracts

Delivery Month		Trading Volume	Deliveries	Deliveries as Percentage of Volume
January	1980	6,410	191	2.98
February	1980	10,603	241	2.27
March	1980	10,259	382	3.72
April	1980	3,563	141	3.96
May	1980	4,845	175	3.61
June	1980	2,354	88	3.74
July	1980	7,135	53	0.74
August	1980	1,984	100	5.04
September	1980	6,830	195	2.86
October	1980	7,209	473	6.56
November	1980	10,454	547	5.23
December	1980	43,490	2,213	5.09
Total	1980	115,136	4,799	4.17
January	1981	60,015	1,341	2.20
February	1981	47,147	1,125	2.40
March	1981	89,737	1,121	1.25
April	1981	41,217	1,027	2.50
May	1981	33,058	440	1.33
June	1981	36,322	667	1.84
July	1981	75,528	777	1.03
August	1981	55,583	418	0.75
September	1981	85,252	1,306	1.53
October	1981	48,317	2,340	4.84
November	1981	52,562	2,339	4.45
December	1981	186,710	2,685	1.14
Total	1981	811,448	15,586	1.92

Source: Compiled from New York Mercantile Exchange data.

Trading in No. 2 was boosted by the elimination of federal price controls on oil in February 1981. Price deregulation meant that the No. 2 contract could be used to hedge other petroleum products. In addition, the unseasonably warm winter in 1979 and unexpected strong conservation efforts by consumers had already demonstrated that fuel prices could actually decrease. For most of the mid-1970s, such price behavior had not been considered possible, and the scarcity of brave souls willing to assume short positions in gas-oil futures was an important factor in the demise of earlier contracts.

A number of state governmental agencies employed the NYMEX No. 2 contract as a hedging device in 1981. In particular, during the summer, the American Refining Company won the contract to supply 17 million gallons of diesel oil to

Table 10-2
No. 2 Heating-Oil Prices
(dollars per gallon)

Quarter/Year	Nearby NYMEX	New York Harbor, Spot	National Average to Customers
1/1978		.3781	.3783
2/1978		.3760	.3760
3/1978		.3788	.3807
4/1978	.4300	.4125	.4047
1/1979	.5900	.5712	.5227
2/1979	.8900	.8750	.6480
3/1979	.8400	.8425	.7773
4/1979	.8275	.8550	.8393
1/1980	.7500	.7537	.9440
2/1980	.7600	.7625	.9750
3/1980	.7911	.7925	.9797
4/1980	.9690	.9575	1.0210
1/1981	.9409	.9425	1.2100
2/1981	.9119	.9112	1.2265

Source: Compiled from New York Mercantile Exchange data.

the Washington, D.C. Metropolitan Area Transit Authority (WMATA). The firm's fixed-price bid was accepted, to the chagrin of the other bidders, all of whom proposed fluctuating prices pegged to product or crude prices. American Refining was able to offer a fixed price, which saved WMATA an estimated $2 million over twelve months, by hedging large volumes of diesel against No. 2 NYMEX contracts.

State and city transportation agencies in Massachusetts and California also have hedged oil futures on the Merc. Massachusetts has begun to require fixed-price bids for No. 2 fuel-oil sales to the state, encouraging prospective suppliers to hedge with futures contracts. California enacted legislation, effective January 1, 1982, expressly permitting the Southern California Rapid Transit District and the San Diego Transportation Corporation to trade in No. 2 contracts on the New York exchange. In both instances, the intention is to use the contracts to hedge against price changes in diesel fuel.

New York Harbor Delivery: Contract Terms

The New York Harbor area includes facilities in the lower Hudson River south of Fort Lee, New Jersey; the East River west of Hunts Point; Upper and Lower

New Jersey Bays; Newark Bay; and the waterways between New Jersey and Staten Island. To qualify as a designated delivery-point, a facility must have a minimum access draft of twenty feet at mean low water to accommodate barges and must have racks for buyers who choose to accept delivery by truck. In addition to No. 2 oil, NYMEX has New York contracts in No. 6 oil (although this contract is inactive) and regular leaded and unleaded gasoline.

The product delivered, in the case of No. 2, must have an API gravity of at least $30°$ and a sulfur content of not more than 0.20 percent. The No. 6 oil contract calls for an API gravity of between $10°$ and $30°$ and a maximum sulfur content of .30 percent. (Additional product specifications are found in section 150.03 of the NYMEX contract, a copy of which is included in appendix E. The contracts specify delivery of 42,000 U.S. gallons (1,000 barrels). Actual physical transference may be between 37,900 gallons (950 barrels) and 44,100 gallons (1,050 barrels)—that is, within plus or minus 5 percent of the contract amount. In the event of delivery of other than the standard amount, an appropriate adjustment is made in the total price paid by the buyer. In the case of a transfer of title when there is no actual physical movement of stocks, delivery must be for exactly 42,000 gallons. Delivery may be made by any of seven methods (depending upon the capabilities and regulations of the facilities involved): barge, truck, tanker; pipeline; intra-facility transfer; inter-facility transfer; or book transfer of title.

NYMEX petroleum futures are traded in what is known as the oil pit on the floor of the Commodity Exchange Center, a commodities- futures trading facility in New York's World Trade Center complex shared by Commodity Exchange (COMEX), Coffee, Sugar, and Cocoa Exchange (CSCE), New York Cotton Exchange (NYCEX), and NYMEX. No. 2 contracts, which trade for delivery in all twelve months, are traded between 10:30 a.m. and 2:45 p.m., New York local time. No. 6 contracts are traded between 10:35 a.m. and 2:43 p.m. EST.

The minimum contract price fluctuation is one point, which is 1/100 of one U.S. cent (U.S. $.0001) per gallon, or $4.20 per contract. The basic maximum price change allowed daily is 2 cents per gallon ($.02), or $840 per contract. If the settlement price on any day varies in either direction from the preceding day's settlement price by two cents per gallon then the maximum permissible fluctuation is increased for the following day to three cents per gallon or $1,260 per contract. If on the following day the settlement price again varies by the maximum limit, the maximum change allowed for the next day is increased to four cents ($.04) per gallon, or $1,680 per contract. The new limit of four cents remains in effect until the settlement price changes from the previous day's closing price by less than that maximum allowed fluctuation. When this occurs, the original maximum of two cents per gallon once again is imposed.

The trading of any contract is stopped on the last business day of the month preceding that contract's delivery month. The delivery procedure begins by noon of the first business day of the delivery month. By that time, the clearing members of the exchange must notify the clearinghouse of the names and commitments of their customers who are under obligation to deliver or accept delivery pursuant to the outstanding matured contracts. The clearing facility then matches buyers and sellers, according to the size of their commitments and, by 9:00 a.m. of the second business day of the delivery month, notifies each of the name of the party to whom they have been matched.

By 4:30 p.m. of the fifth business day of the delivery month, the clearing member who is buying must submit written instructions to the clearinghouse specifying the method by which and the day (or period of days) on which he will accept delivery. If he desires, at this time the buyer may also designate a firm to carry out quality and quantity inspections of the seller's product. After the clearing facility receives these instructions from the buyer, it relays them to the seller. If the buyer has not requested a quantity inspection, the seller may appoint someone to do this.

Delivery must be made between the fifth business day and the last business day of the delivery month. The buyer then is required to furnish a certified check for full payment to the seller by noon on the day after delivery. If there are payment adjustments to be made, they must be completed by noon on the third business day of that month. If a contract is settled by more than one delivery, each shipment requires separate payment. All deliveries are FOB at the facility where the seller's product is stored. The seller is responsible for all taxes and fees related to the product until the actual time of delivery.

An Exchange of Futures for Product (EFP) is a mechanism that allows a matched buyer and seller to transact business between themselves according to terms different from those specified by the NYMEX contract. Such differences can include the place of delivery, the price at which the transaction will be concluded, or the date of delivery, among others. To arrange for such a consummation of a transaction, the parties to the trade must notify the clearinghouse by the second to last business day of the delivery month of the conditions under which they wish to conclude their transaction. They must also report to the exchange on the validity of the transaction and prove that a change in ownership has been effected.

Gulf Coast Delivery of No. 2 Oil: Contract Terms

In August 1981, NYMEX began trading a No. 2 futures contract for delivery at various points on the coast of the Gulf of Mexico. All of the delivery points are located between Pasadena, Texas and Collins, Mississippi and have access to the Colonial pipeline, which extends from Texas to New Jersey. These ports must have a draft of at least thirty feet to accomodate tankers. While New York and the Northeast comprise a consumer center of many petroleum products, the Gulf Coast is the primary refining center of the country and is the major point-of entry for imported oil. Accordingly, there is a great deal of buying and selling in the area. Refiners sell some of their product to local consumers, rather than transport it to other parts of the country, large commercial consumers operating in the Gulf region buy product there, and distributors and traders buy and sell for themselves and as agents for others.

The Gulf Coast contract is basically identical to the New York Harbor contract, except for some details about the actual delivery of product. For example, all deliveries are made at the price stipulated by the contract, except for those made by Colonial Pipeline at Beaumont and Port Arthur, Texas; at Lake Charles and Baton Rouge, Louisiana; and at Collins, Mississippi. The price paid if delivery is at one of these points must include an amount to compensate for the tariffs charged by the Colonial Pipeline Company. Deliveries by Colonial Pipeline must be made during the second or third cycle—generally the eleventh day through the last day—of the delivery month.

Product specifications are the same as the New York contract. This permits easy arbitrage between the Gulf Coast and New York contracts. Appendix F contains a copy of the Gulf Coast No. 2 contract.

Gasoline-Futures Contracts

In October 1981, the New York Merc began trading futures contracts for leaded and unleaded regular gasoline, with delivery in New York Harbor. Similar contracts for delivery in the Gulf Coast area were opened for trading three weeks later.

The gasoline contracts, which trade for all months, are each for 42,000 U.S. gallon (1,000 barrel) lots, with a volume tolerance of plus or minus 5 percent, and appropriate total cost adjustments in the event of actual delivery. Book transfers are for exactly 42,000 gallons.

The unleaded regular contract specifies 87 octane minimum and maximum of 0.03 grams of lead per gallon. The leaded contract requires a minimum octane rating of 89, and a maximum lead content of 4.0 grams per gallon. Other technical specifications may be found in the contracts in appendix F.

Delivery is by truck, barge, tanker, pipeline, inter-facility or intra-facility transfer, or by book transfer. The permissible price fluctuations and the delivery procedures are the same as those for the No. 2 heating-oil contract.

11 International Petroleum Exchange

The Founding of a New Exchange

The International Petroleum Exchange began trading gas-oil futures in London in April 1981. The IPE has been much heralded, in Britain at least, as a long-overdue response to the turbulent world petroleum market. While there was some preliminary talk in Europe of futures trading in petroleum products in 1973 and 1974, and the idea periodically resurfaced, conditions postponed the creation of a petroleum futures market. The market tremors caused by the Iranian revolution finally stimulated serious talk about the formation of futures contracts for petroleum products. After some two years of detailed planning, the London exchange opened its doors.

The increasing decentralization of the world petroleum industry since 1974 has created an important precondition for successful futures trading: a competitive market with many independent and non-integrated refiners, distributors, and traders. The IPE, moreover, was inspired by the successful launch of trade in No. 2 heating-oil futures by the New York Merc in 1978. The New York contract proved that futures trading in No. 2 oil could work and provided an example for the London Exchange and European traders.

London is a natural center for the futures trade in oil products. The city has a rich history in futures trading that dates back more than a century, and it is the center of the European oil trade. London traders are, therefore, uniquely familiar with the worlds of both petroleum and commodity futures. The city, of course, commands the communications and financial infrastructures necessary for the petroleum-futures trade. Moreover, it is close to the Rotterdam market and in a time zone that permits trade with the European continent and the East in the morning and with the United States and the rest of the Western hemisphere in the late afternoon.

The founders of the IPE hope to diversify into futures trading in a host of other petroleum products, possibly including crude oil. There has been talk of developing contracts in as many as a dozen other products, with most debate centering on naphtha, benzene, gasoline, bunker oil, and jet fuels. The decision to test the European petroleum futures-market with a gas-oil contract was a good one. Gas oil accounts for about half of the Rotterdam trade and enjoys widespread demand. The product, moreover, is subject to seasonal fluctuation in production and demand related to refinery output of gasoline and temperature changes. Therefore, gas oil displays instabilities of both supply and demand

95

and in price that make it especially appropriate for futures trading. The apparent success of the N.Y. Merc's futures contract in No. 2 oil also indicated that gas oil was the best first choice of product to trade.

The IPE, like any new market, was greeted with a mixture of anticipation, suspicion, and apathy. Traders in other commodity futures were optimistic about the petroleum futures trade both on its own merits and as a potential hedging device. There was also hope that the new gas-oil contract would revive interest in futures trading in other commodities, many of which were suffering through a sluggish period. Yet, many oil traders and firms, the larger in particular, displayed a reluctance to become associated with an uncertain enterprise that might change the structure of the oil market in unknown ways. Unaccustomed to using a futures market, the oil professionals were wary of the purported advantages to be gained by trading. Primarily, they did not feel that it was a necessary adjunct to their operations. Many still prefer to rely on trading methods that do not involve futures.

The founders of the IPE knew they had a real problem in gaining acceptance for the new market from the oil industry, and they mapped a detailed plan in advance of the scheduled opening in April 1981. There was wide publicity in a campaign that stressed education. The interested and the curious were invited to learn about futures trading and the IPE; exhibits explained the advantages of the futures market.

The careful preparation appears to have been well worth it. While the IPE is still too young to permit a sure prediction of the future, it appears to have the vitality necessary for success. Turnover on opening day was 2,800 lots (1.8 million tonnes), more than anyone expected. Average daily turnover has averaged approximately 900 lots. This is less than one tenth of the volume of No. 2 oil trading in the New York Merc, but is considerably more than that traded when the Merc contract was first introduced. Even accounting for the larger volume of a single Merc contract in No. 2, turnover on the IPE has exceeded that for the early months of the Merc and is more than sufficient to maintain the health of the exchange during its infancy. IPE spokespeople are confident not only that the exchange will succeed, but also that it will become a leading London commodities market.

The Contract

The IPE gas-oil contract is for one hundred tonnes of product. The contract is denominated in U.S. dollars, and payment is to be made in the same currency in London. Prices are determined by open outcry. The minimum price-fluctuation is twenty-five cents per tonne, and the minimum price is thirty dollars per tonne. Whenever the price moves by thirty dollars in either direction from the previous day's closing price, trading is suspended for thirty minutes, after which time trading resumes without limits for the remainder of the day.

Delivery is designated at specified tank installations in the Amsterdam-Rotterdam-Antwerp area. Delivery takes place between the fourteenth and the last day of the contract month, at the option of the seller. Contract rates are *ex tank,* meaning that seller is responsible for costs incurred in pumping oil out.

Trading for each delivery month ends at 3:30 p.m. on the last business day of the month preceding delivery. After that time, the International Commodity Clearing House (the ICCH is the clearing facility for the IPE) informs holders of open contracts of their respective obligations. The ICCH guarantees supply in the event a seller cannot make delivery. Trading is for nine consecutive months, including the current month. Contracts can be traded up to nine months ahead, after which they can be renegotiated.

The contract size (100 tonnes) is noticeably small compared to the needs of large users and traders and the regular Rotterdam trade. The barge market averages about 6,000 tonnes per load, while cargoes are approximately 30,000 tonnes. As contracts can be traded readily in multiple lots, consumers and traders with larger demands simply must buy more contracts (assuming availability of supply). On the other hand, the small quantity contract was devised to attract speculators and small-trade users of product. By being able to satisfy both major and minor traders and consumers, the IPE contract can increase the breadth of the market.

Membership

Reliance on the open outcry necessarily limits the number of floor members of the exchange. The composition of floor membership has been particularly important to the IPE's chances of success. With a limit of thirty-five floor members, the IPE has attracted firms with the right degree of expertise in the particular commodity and its trade, and in futures trading in general.

Floor members (see appendix F for a list of floor and trade members) must maintain a London office, have a net minimum worth of £20,000. As a floor member, a firm enjoys full voting rights and can trade on the IPE free of commission.

To accommodate those companies that wish to retain their anonymity by trading through a floor member and not incure the costs of maintaining a London office and floor trading-staff, there is trade membership. Trade members need a minimum net worth of £100,000 and must be established companies with an ongoing interest in the world oil trade. The trade membership fee is £5,000. Trade members do not have voting rights but can trade at a lower rate of commission than non-memberships of the IPE.

Firms that do not qualify for trade membership can be general members, provided they meet some minimum qualifications. This form of membership is designed primarily to satisfy speculators on the market. All members of the IPE, regardless of class of membership, must pass all business through the floor of the exchange.

London and New York

Although the New York oil-futures trade is better established than the London trade, the two markets have a type of symbiotic relationship. A number of U.S. firms are trade members of the IPE, and a handful of U.S. companies maintain floor membership through their London subsidiaries.

The London market opens five hours ahead of its New York counterpart, giving U.S. observers an indicator of price direction and magnitude. The linkage between Rotterdam and New York prices make the IPE an important leading indicator of trade and price movements in New York later in the day.

Obviously, the greatest interrelationship between New York and London will be based on arbitrage. To expedite arbitrage, direct communications lines have been installed between the IPE and the New York Merc.

Contract similarities, including the use of U.S. dollars, also should encourage the arbitrage trade. Some analysts have suggested that differences in sulfur content and quantity, however, will hinder arbitrage. The New York contract specifies a minimum sulfur content of 0.2 percent by weight, while the London contract allows for 0.3 percent. The IPE's contract, furthermore, is for 100 tonnes, while the Merc's is for 42,000 U.S. gallons (approximately 138 tonnes).

These differences are really minor. While a product must be deliverable to be useful in futures trading, the small percentage of contracts that actually culminate in physical delivery means that such small variations as exist between the New York and London contracts do not significantly interfere with arbitrage.

The quantity differential also is largely irrelevant. While single lots are not equal in quantity, multiple lots can be traded to approach parity. Five New York Merc lots, for example, would be only 1.5 percent less by weight than seven lots on the IPE. The arbitrageur would purchase lots not on a one-to-one basis, but with the goal of acquiring equivalent quantities. Cash payments could be calculated to account for quantity differences.

12 Possible Futures in Other Products

Continued uncertainties about world petroleum prices and the successful introduction of futures trading in heating oil in both London and New York have stimulated interest in the possibility of futures trading in other petroleum products.

Other petroleum products that have been mentioned or are being launched now include heavy fuel oils, naphthas, motor gasolines, aviation gasolines, and liquified petroleum gases. Therefore, we offer a brief discussion of each of these products and some thoughts concerning their potential for futures trading.

Heavy Fuel Oil

Description

Heavy fuel oils are what is left after gases and distillates have been boiled off during the refining process. These fractions are too heavy to vaporize when heated under atmospheric pressure and include any inorganic ash compounds or metals in the crude. They also are too heavy to burn without another fuel with which to start. Commercial grades of residual fuel oils are designated as Nos. 4, 5, and 6 oils, depending upon their specific gravity. No. 6 oil is the most dense and the most commonly used, mainly as a boiler fuel to raise steam for generating electricity. Residual fuels also include bunker fuels used by ships.

Some technical processes have been developed to remove the metals in heavy oils. Additives also help reduce the accumulation of sludge and the tendency for deposits to develop, as well as prevent corrosion and increase combustion efficiency. Because of the increased environmental concern of recent years, advances that have been made toward decreasing the sulfur content of this fuel.

Uses

Heavy fuel oils are used in the commercial, industrial, and marine sectors for space heating and electric power generation. Residual oils are particularly appropriate where large volumes of fuel are needed, such as for electricity, industrial steam raising, process heating, and ship propulsion. Because it is viscous, residual fuel requires preheating facilities that improve the oil's ability to flow.

Most of the major consumers of heavy fuel oil use No. 6 grade oil. This is cheaper than the lower viscosity oils, which are blended with a lighter and, therefore, more expensive stock to lower their pour point. Bunker fuel, known as Bunker C, is the marine equivalent to No. 6 oil.

For many years, residual oil (resid) had significant advantages over coal as a fuel, including cost, impact on the environment, and ease of storage. Today, the cost advantage held by residual fuels has been eroded by the increase in oil prices and, in some areas, by the strict limits on acceptable sulfur content. Nuclear fuels also compete with heavy oils in the production of electricity.

Supply and Demand

While the use of residual oil as a heating fuel shows predictable seasonal variations, its use as an industrial fuel is a good barometer of industrial activity. Consumption of heavy fuel oil by industry and utilities will change in sympathy with the business cycle. Residual-oil consumption in Western Europe and the United States, for example, declined during the recessions of 1973–1975 and 1978–1981.

Residual fuel oil prices may also reflect, to some extent, fluctuations in world shipping volumes and costs. This tends to be especially true for the United States, where refineries optimize their gasoline output and avoid making resid. Therefore, considerable volumes of heavy fuel-oil are imported. The United States imports over one third of its heavy fuel-oil needs. In Western Europe and Japan as well, refiners are minimizng the production of residual oils, but supply will continue to outpace demand for at least the rest of the 1980s.

Since 1973, resid consumption in the industrial nations has been declining in absolute terms, lowering its percentage share of total oil consumption. This trend seems likely to continue as consumers substitute other fuels. In the United States, the use of residual oils peaked in 1977 and has been falling ever since, as industries convert to natural gas or gas oil and power plants opt for coal. This decline has been accelerated by dropping demand for bunker fuel, as fewer tankers are needed for imports.

Potential for Futures Trading

While heavy fuel oil prices can move in parallel to light heating oil, variations in supply and demand can disrupt this apparent link. As a result, consumers and producers of residual oils are limited in the extent to which they can hedge their purchases and sales by trading futures in No. 2 heating oil. Trading resid futures on their own has some real appeal. For instance, the sensitivity of tanker rates to international disturbances and the impacts of tanker movements on United States fuel-oil prices, even if marginal, offer conditions of potential price instability to make resid-futures trading highly interesting.

Futures trading in No. 6 fuel-oil contracts, stipulating New York Harbor area delivery, was introduced by the New York Mercantile Exchange in August 1978. While this contract is still technically available, trade in No. 6 oil is not active. An earlier effort by the Merc to trade No. 6 oil, launched in October 1974 with Rotterdam delivery, also floundered. The buying and selling of futures in No. 6 oil has remained sluggish for several reasons, the most important of which is the small number of buyers and sellers of this fuel. Unlike No. 2 heating oil, which is sold in the United States through 12,000 to 18,000 jobbers, No. 6 oil is sold primarily by refineries, or by their marketing subsidiaries, directly to the utilities or large industrial users. In some cases, it is sold through bidding. Without enough market participants, the need for a futures market is eliminated.

It has also been suggested that the ability of utilities, the largest consumers of fuel oil in the United States, to pass on fuel cost increases to consumers in the form of higher electricity rates, may dampen their incentive to engage in futures trading to protect themselves against price increases. In a time of uncertain and rising energy costs, that is a secondary factor behind the lackadaisical activity in No. 6 oil-futures markets, although it could partially explain the reluctance of utilities to pursue futures trading.

Another factor that may have dampened active trading in No. 6 fuel has been the product specifications of the NYMEX contract. In accordance with New York City law, the contract limits the maximum allowable sulfur content to 0.3 percent, a stricter requirement than is imposed in most other areas. This disparity may inhibit the buying of No. 6 futures, with their New York delivery, owing to the cost differential between high- and low-sulfur fuels. Although only a small percentage of contracts traded on any futures market are settled by physical delivery, those traders that do want delivery are reluctant to use the NYMEX market. Generally speaking, sulfur differentials are only a side issue in deferring trade.

The relatively small number of buyers and sellers of residual oil poses a very significant obstacle to successful futures trading in No. 6. The outlook will not improve as consumption of heavy fuel oil in both the United States and Western Europe is expected to keep declining in the 1980s. Conversion to the use of other fuels by utilities and other end-users is likely to continue, further shrinking the pool of potential buyers and sellers. In the United States, demand for heavy fuel oil as a percentage of the petroleum barrel is expected to decline from 17 percent in 1980 to only 10% to 15% in 1990, and in Western Europe, a similar trend is likely. The consumption of heavy fuel oil is expected by most industry observers to fall steadily throughout the 1980s and 1990s.

All things considered, there does not appear to be enough enthusiasm for futures trading in No. 6 heating oil for a satisfactory level of futures trading in that product ever to be reached.

Gasoline

Gasoline is used everywhere and is known by many names: mogas, motor spirit, and petrol. It is a light distillate with a boiling range of $30°$ C. to $200°$ C. Gasoline is colorless, volatile, and highly flammable. For a century, it has been the fuel in spark-ignition internal-combustion engines.

Commercial gasoline contains various hydrocarbons, selectively blended to achieve an effective level of engine performance. Most research on oil refining, leading to units such as catalytic reformers and crackers, was done to find ways to convert crude-oil fractions to gasoline.

Various technical specifications determine the rating of a gasoline and indicate the performance level of the fuel. Some of the more important of these are specific gravity, boiling range, and octane rating.

Octane ratings (regular or premium) determine the grade of gasoline that is traded. The octane level, which indicates the knocking tendencies, is the most important quality of a gasoline. Octane ratings measure the percentage of iso-octane present in the gasoline. Iso-octane has an assigned octane rating of 100. The lower the percentage of iso-octane, the lower the octane rating. Premium gasolines have higher octane ratings, and cost more to make than regular gasolines.

Supply and Demand

Petroleum refining pivots around the demand for and the supply of gasoline, which is the refiner's most profitable product. This is true everywhere, although the gasoline cut in U.S. refineries is much greater than it is in Europe. Average refinery yields of gasoline, by volume, for North America are about 45 percent, as compared to about 25 percent in Western Europe, which predominantly reflects the role of cars and trucks in the United States.

The pattern of supply and demand for gasoline is strongly seasonal and is inversely related to that for heating oil. Demand for gasoline is up in the motoring season, from late spring through early fall. Refiners and distributors build up stocks in late winter and early spring, and draw down inventories in the late summer and early fall.

Futures Trading

During most of the 1970s, the major obstacle in the United States to the establishment of futures trading in gasoline was price controls. In anticipation of the previously announced schedule of price decontrol, the New York Mercantile Exchange applied to the Commodities Futures Trading Commission for permission to begin trading in gasoline. With the lifting of crude-oil price controls by President Reagan in February 1981, the introduction of futures trading was speeded and NYMEX introduced a leaded and unleaded gasoline contract during the first week of October 1981. Buyers and sellers of gasoline now can take advantage of the rough price relationship between No. 2 heating oil and gasoline as a hedging strategy and engage in interproduct arbitrage. Refiners, moreover, can hedge some 70 percent of their crude-oil runs by using heating oil and gasoline futures.

The NYMEX contract is for 1,000 barrel lots (42,000 U.S. gallons), with New York and Gulf Coast delivery for leaded and unleaded gasoline. In light of the success of the No. 2 heating-oil contract, the prospects for healthy trading of gasoline futures look good. For one, the size of the gasoline market is much bigger than that for No. 2 oil. In the United States, demand for gasoline averaged 6.6 million barrels per day in 1980, as compared to only 2.9 million barrels per day for distillate heating oil. Also, the number of middlemen, jobbers, traders, and the like involved in the introduction and marketing of gasoline—that is the number of potential market participants—is greater than for No. 2 heating oil. There are some 20,000 U.S. independent marketers and 200,000 service station owners, in addition to thousands of car fleet owners and trucking firms, that can benefit from trading in gasoline futures. Thus, there is a large enough pool of buyers and sellers to more than ensure the viability of gasoline-futures trading. The potential futures-trade in gasoline, in fact, is considerably larger than that in No. 2 oil.

There are other factors as well which indicate the promise of strong futures trading in gasoline. The impact of seasonality on supply and demand, and the corresponding build-up and draw-down of inventories, creates a strong incentive for those in the industry to trade futures as a way to provide price protection and profits. It is easy to establish a standard set of specifications for gasoline-futures trading. The obstacles presented by the differences in sulfur content for No. 6 oil that are allowed in various parts of the United States do not exist for gasoline.

As the most valuable and largest segment of the barrel, gasoline prices are closely watched by producers, traders, and consumers. Table 12-1 summarizes leaded and unleaded gasoline prices in New York and the United States since 1978. These data indicate the volatility of spot and retail prices, a favorable condition for an effective futures trade.

Table 12-1
New York City and U.S. Gasoline Prices
(dollars per gallon)

Quarter/Year	Spot, New York City Leaded	Spot, New York City Unleaded	Retail, U.S. City Leaded	Retail, U.S. City Unleaded
1/1978	.3686	.3873	.617	.658
2/1978	.4021	.4222	.634	.678
3/1978	.4545	.4809	.658	.702
4/1978	.5037	.5334	.675	.717
1/1979	.6716	.7021	.706	.755
2/1979	1.0513	1.0867	.856	.901
3/1979	.8570	.8852	.973	1.020
4/1979	1.1531	1.1840	1.018	1.065
1/1980	.9374	.9507	1.202	1.252
2/1980	.9106	.9232	1.217	1.269
3/1980	.8664	.9115	1.197	1.257
4/1980	.9275	.9606	1.197	1.258
1/1981	.9872	1.0177	1.352	1.417
2/1981	.9729	1.0215	1.324	1.391

Source: Compiled from New York Mercantile Exchange data.

Some people think that available storage capacity for gasoline is too small to support a large volume of futures trade, if many buyers take final delivery of the product. On the NYMEX, however, only about 1 to 3 percent of the total trade in No. 2 heating oil has resulted in actual delivery of the product, and for most futures markets the figure is under 5 percent. It seems probable that a gasoline-futures market would be used primarily as a financial mechanism, rather than as a source of product for final delivery. Storage capacity should be adequate.

It is likely that contracts for both leaded and unleaded gasoline will be traded in approximately equal volumes, for a few years. There is now a balance in the use of these two types of fuel in the United States. Unleaded gas accounted for about 52 percent of consumption in 1981, and the market share of unleaded gasoline should rise steadily throughout the 1980s, maybe reaching 75 percent by the end of the decade, as older cars are phased out.

Naphtha

One of the sleepers that could become a candidate for futures trading is naphtha, a widely-used petrochemical feedstock. Naphtha is sometimes referred to as *heavy benzene* or *heavy gasoline*. The twenty-four-member nation Organization for Economic Cooperation and Development (OECD), defines naphthas as including those "light hydrocarbons boiling predominantly below 200°C.... normally with an octane volume too low to permit use as a spark ignition engine fuel."

Naphtha is employed in a number of ways. In a refinery, the liquid streams going into gasolines and kerosenes are actually naphthas. In addition to its role as a blending agent in gasolines, and as a petrochemical feedstock, naphtha is an industrial solvent. Aliphatic naphthas are low in odor, toxicity, and solvent power. This makes them appropriate for dry cleaning, for processing soybeans, and for other jobs where only moderate solvent power is called for. Aromatic naphthas, on the other hand, have a high solvency and are used mainly as thinners and carriers for paints. The solvent power of naphthas makes them extremely valuable to the rubber industry, to the leather industry for degreasing skins, and to the metal industry for cleaning metals. They are also used in insecticides and weed killers, floor and furniture waxes, and shoe polishes.

Prospects for Futures Trading

Clearly, naphtha has a variety of end markets, and its widespread use by various industries fulfills one of the basic criteria necessary to the successful operation of a futures market. Likewise, the production of naphtha by many refineries ensures a diversified source of supply. But is the establishment of futures trading in naphtha viable?

As a petroleum product, the price of naphtha is linked to the supply uncertainties and price volatility common to the oil business. The importance of this product to a divergent number of industries, and particularly its importance as a major feedstock for the petrochemical industry, provides a strong incentive for industrial users to hedge purchases.

Naphtha sold for under $20 per tonne twenty years ago, but more recently prices have increased. Spot prices for naphtha soared in European markets in 1979, from about $200 per t at the beginning of the year to about $400 per t one year later, and there was a strong upward pull exerted on contract prices—a vivid illustration of the circumstances under which futures transactions might have been financially advantageous for both buyers and sellers. In 1980, after the big rise of spot prices, five major European chemical producers—Imperial Chemical Industries, DSM, Rhone-Poulenc, BASF, and Bayer—established a reporting system to keep closer track of naphtha pricing. Such detailed pricing data, often termed *transparency of prices,* is one of the benefits characteristic of futures trading.

In the United States, the decontrol of crude-oil prices in February 1981 not only moved naphtha prices up, but also made them more susceptible to sharp price swings. This means naphtha-futures trading is in the financial interest of U.S. users.

Nevertheless, there are some obstacles. The diverse properties of different naphthas probably require standard sets of technical specifications that would be agreeable among end users. By adopting contract terms that provide for a price adjustment when a product differs from the standard specifications, it is conceivable that futures trading in naphtha could develop.

Another possible inhibitor to successful futures-trading in naphtha is the limited effects of seasonality on this product. Without a seasonal build-up and draw-down of stocks, there might be insufficient reason to hedge purchases and sales. Although periods of price volatility certainly provide an incentive for naphtha users and producers to try hedging, using a futures market only in times of abnormal market activity is not enough. A successful market depends upon consistent use.

Like residual fuel-oil, naphtha demand moves in sympathy with international economic activity. So, there may be sufficient fluctuations in supply and demand to make futures trading feasible. It is certainly more attractive as a futures candidate than resid is. Buyers and suppliers abound, and the major question remaining is whether or not it is possible to specify contract standards that are applicable to a wide number of users. Regardless of the specifications, however, if a steady price differential is maintained, it would be a valuable hedging vehicle for all naphtha users.

Liquified Petroleum Gas (LPG)

There are two liquified petroleum gases: propane and butane. Propane and butane are produced from the processing of natural gas and the distillation of crude oil. Being gaseous at atmospheric pressure and ambient atmospheric temperature, LPG must be stored in specially designed pressurized cylinders.

Propane also is referred to as *bottled* or *tank* gas. Although stored in liquid form, it is burned as a gas. Derived mainly from the processing of natural gas and the distillation of crude oil, LPG is a highly efficient fuel that burns clearly.

LPG can be used as a fuel for tractors, trucks, buses, and agricultural equipment, as a feedstock for the chemical industry, and as a fuel for domestic cooking and heating, particularly in rural areas. Other areas, where natural gas pipelines are not available, also often use LPG.

Propane is what most buyers prefer when using LPG as a fuel. Propane has a high energy content. It can fuel engines with high compression ratios. Propane used in internal-combustion engines reduces engine wear, thereby keeping maintenance costs lower and extending engine life longer than possible with gasoline and diesel fuels. It also burns cleanly, with very low emission. LPG can be competitive with both gasoline and diesel fuels in operating costs per mile, but its use requires investing in the conversion of the engine itself so that it can burn propane. Depending upon local laws, LPG taxes tend to be less than those on gasolines. Some of the cost advantages held by propane are undercut by the expense of purchasing specialized handling and storage equipment. Nevertheless, owing to the increasing cost of gasoline, there is a steady but sporadic interest in the conversion of truck and car fleets to LPG use.

In the petrochemical industry, where LPG is widely used, butane can compare favorably both in terms of price and supply with other oil-derived feedstocks, such as naphtha. It is also a good feedstock for ethylene crackers.

Prospects for Futures Trading

A propane contract was introduced on the New York Cotton Exchange in 1971. The contract size was 100,000 gallons, and the delivery point was Mont Belvieu, Texas. This contract, while still extant, became increasingly inactive in recent years and was phased out by the end of 1981. In December 1981, the exchange introduced a new LPG contract (see appendix I). The 1,000 barrel contract has two delivery points, Mont Belvieu, and Conway, Kansas, providing buyers and sellers a choice.

The LPG market holds a good deal of promise. The fuel is cost competitive, with prices running approximately 30 percent lower than those for gasoline. Spot prices for propane are variable, ranging between 16.5 and 66 cents per gallon in 1979 and between 39.2 cents and 56.3 cents per gallon in 1980. Spot prices for these two years are given in table 12-2. Approximately 90 percent of the LPG consumed in the United States, moreover, is produced domestically, making it economically and politically attractice.

The near-term outlook for world LPG demand is quite buoyant, and there have been predictions of average increases of 10 percent per year in LPG trade throughout the next decade. Although the rate of growth will be somewhat less in the United States because demand is more mature, such an expansion of world trade would help the trading of the propane contract. The use of LPG as a petrochemical feedstock, and the sensitivity of the petrochemicals industry to swings in economic activity, may attract that industry. Car and truck fleets have increasingly been converted to propane, and the Ford Motor Company recently announced its intent to market cars that run on propane. These trends should spark consumption and add to the number of potential participants in the LPG futures market. But it will be a few years yet before this market develops.

Jet Fuels

Jet fuels are a special grade of kerosene designed for use in jet aircraft. They may have methane or naphthene added to them to produce a lower flash point for

Table 12-2
Mt. Belvieu, Texas: Propane Spot Prices
(cents per gallon)

1979	*Price*	*1980*	*Price*
January	16.5	January	53.0
February	18.5	February	46.5
March	20.5	March	44.6
April	25.5	April	48.6
May	35.0	May	47.0
June	40.6	June	43.8
July	36.0	July	39.2
August	37.6	August	39.7
September	48.0	September	42.4
October	48.7	October	48.5
November	55.0	November	56.3
December	56.0	December	49.0

Source: Compiled from New York Cotton Exchange data.

military aircraft engines. The naphtha-kerosene blend used by the U.S. Air Force is known as JP-4 (or commercially as Jet B fuel). The U.S. Navy uses a kerosene fuel known as JP-5. Airlines use Jet A, or Jet A-1, fuel. Jet A kerosene has a lower freezing point, which makes it more suitable for use as a long-haul trans-oceanic flight fuel, while the slightly higher freezing point of Jet A-1 fuel makes it better for use in shorter, overland flights.

The consumption of jet fuels must conform to strict specifications. These fuels must burn cleanly, producing no gum or resin deposits to interfere with the operation of the jet engine. They also must have much higher octane levels than automobile gasoline. Anti-knock control is also important. In addition to providing the energy to power the plane, jet fuels must also serve as a coolant for aviation lubricating-oil during the flight.

Supply and Demand

Civilian consumption is relatively high for Jet A and A-1 fuel, and is less so for Jet B fuels. For jet fuels as a group, overall U.S. demand is predicted to grow by more than 50 percent by the year 2000, according a cross-section of recent industry forecasts.

Although passenger use of airlines is seasonal, this is not reflected in the demand for jet fuels, because it is the capacity levels, rather than the number of flights, that are substantially affected. While there is some correspondence between the overall level of economic activity and the demand for jet fuel, it is not too significant.

Prospects for Futures Trading

The demand for jet fuel in the United States during 1980 was slightly less than 1.1 million barrels per day as compared to 6.6 million barrels per day for gasoline, and almost 2.9 million barrels per day for distillate fuel oil. The number of buyers of jet fuels are limited, and the needs of most of these are met primarily through long-term contracts with refiners. Outside of these long-term contracts, there are a few spot-market sales. When these spot sales do occur, they are at above-contract prices, reflecting the urgent need of the buyer for immediate delivery of fuel. There were occasional spot shortages of jet fuels in the United States during the price controls of the late 1970s, when frantic scrambling to meet airline needs was very often the order of the day. These factors, in addition to the lack of seasonal impacts on inventories, are significant barriers to futures trading in jet fuels. Another real barrier to jet-kerosene futures trading is the high product-quality standards. Jet fuel is fragile; it picks up water easily and cannot be used if contaminated. Airlines like dealing with assured supply sources, and might not wish to take chances with deliveries from anyone but established suppliers. There is some price correlation, however, between No. 2 heating oil and jet fuels, which offers the airline industry a hedging vehicle against volatile energy prices in the absence of a futures contract for jet fuels.

**Part IV
International Issues**

13 Prospects for Crude-Oil Futures

Albert L. Danielsen

Analysts do not unanimously agree about the criteria that should be used to predict the success of a new futures contract. Prerequisites have included characteristics of the commodity itself, such as storability, measurability, and homogeneity, as well as its being a basic commodity. Other characteristics are those related to the size and competitiveness of the market. It has been contended that a highly competitive market will promote price variability and a desire for hedging among members of the trade. In addition, a broadly-based market, free of government regulation and state trading, will attract speculators and thus provide liquidity and a more efficient market.

How does crude oil measure up against these criteria? It is obviously basic, measurable, and storable, but it is not a homogeneous commodity. Crude-oil markets are among the largest in the world, but they are subject to numerous government regulations and extensive state trading. If all of the previously mentioned conditions are required for a viable futures-market, then crude oil obviously does not qualify. More recent appraisals of the conditions necessary for futures trading, however, have been less restrictive. More emphasis is placed on the use of futures as a risk-management tool.

The potential for crude-oil futures trading depends on its use as a tool in managing risk associated with temporal price variations. The need to manage risk through futures depends on trade practices and market structure. This chapter will focus on market structure and contractual arrangements in crude-oil trade; chapter 14 will consider the impact of crude-oil and refined-product futures trading on the structure and performance of petroleum markets.

Characteristics of the Crude-Oil Market

Broad Base of the Crude-Oil Market

Crude oil is the most important commodity in world trade as measured by tonnage and market value. In 1979, 3.2 billion tonnes of oil were produced, an amount exceeded only by coal at 3.7 billion tonnes. Combined production of the principal agricultural commodities, wheat, corn, and soybeans, was less than one billion metric tonnes. Crude oil has a far greater market value and enters into international trade more extensively than coal and other commodities. Oil accounts for about one-half of the tonnage and two-thirds of the tonne-kilometers shipped in ocean-going carriers. Oil is more easily transported than coal and at a lower cost because it is a liquid and contains half again as many BTUs per unit of measure. In addition, its efficiency in combustion is greater than that of coal. All these factors enhance its value to ultimate consumers.

Oil is by far the most important commodity in the world as measured by market value. The value of the following commodities was calculated by multiplying 1979 FOB prices by total world production:

Commodity	Market Value FOB Billions of U.S. Dollars
Energy	
Crude Oil	$424
Coal	100
Grains	
Wheat	56
Corn	35
Soybean meal	20
Precious Metals	
Gold	13
Silver	4

The crude-oil market obviously meets the test of being broadly based. It is by far the most broadly based market in the world.

Market Performance

Price volatility is the primary characteristic that makes a commodity a suitable candidate for futures trading. Price stability or low volatility in commodity markets limit risk and largely negate the desire to hedge or speculate. Until the early 1970s, any proposal to devise a contract sensitive to oil price changes would have been rejected on the grounds of insufficient price variability.

Prices were remarkably stable in the United States during the period of 1949 to 1972 because of prorationing by the state regulatory authorities and the 1959 Mandatory Oil Import Control Program. Prices were also fairly stable on world markets until 1959 because they were pegged to U.S. prices. The international majors used informal prorationing to limit output and maintain prices on a world scale. Their efforts were only partially successful, as prices declined steadily from 1959 until the Teheran-Tripoli Agreements in early 1971. The decline was so gradual, however, that there was relatively little money at risk for potential hedgers and little to be made by speculators.

Market Structure

The structure of crude-oil markets changed slowly during the 1950s and 1960s. In general, the member countries of OPEC gained a greater degree of control over pricing and output decisions, largely at the expense of the international majors. In addition, independent and national oil companies have come to play a more important role. These changes resulted in volatile spot prices and an upward ratcheting of contract prices during the 1970s. In order to understand and assess these changes, it is necessary to examine the principal participants in oil markets and their relative influence.

Market Participants

Until the 1960s, most oil production was controlled at the source by the international majors, which were integrated from the wellhead to the pump. Oil was produced through concession arrangements with the host governments or purchased on long-term contracts. There was very little spot trading. During this period, the majors were effectively their own insurers against risks associated with price variability.

The dominant position of the international majors was increasingly eroded by Importing-Country National Oil Companies (INOCs), independent oil companies, and the Exporting-Country National Oil Companies (ENOCs). During the 1960s, the exporting-country governments invited the independents to bid for concessions and lift oil in competition with the majors. This created excess capacity that effectively held crude-oil prices down. Excess capacity was brought onstream when a supply disruption occurred, such as the 1967 Six-Day War and when weather or business conditions placed inordinate demands on the delivery system.

During the 1960s, and especially the 1970s, the ENOCs increased their participation in such upstream activities as production and ocean transport. The ENOCs also sought a larger role in refining and marketing. The INOCs, which have traditionally been involved in downstream activities of refining and marketing, now seek greater security of supply through state trading and/or exploration and production on their own account. The independents continue to make inroads when and where they can. These developments are a threat to the integrated majors that must constantly move over to accommodate newcomers, yield market shares at all levels of the delivery system, or more actively compete and erode profit margins.

Contractual Relations. The most direct, recurrent, and important interrelations among the principal actors in world petroleum markets are between public officials in the ministries of petroleum (or ENOCs) in producing countries and representatives of the international oil companies. The latter include the majors, independents, and INOCs. The majors remain the most important of these groups. Financial relations with international banks are also important but ancillary to petroleum markets. The relations among representatives of the exporting countries and international oil companies are in general orderly, well structured, and governed by international law. From the standpoint of crude-oil futures trading, the most important contractual relations are those related to the initial acquisition of crude oil.

The ministries of petroleum and/or ENOCs contract with the international majors and independents to produce the bulk of all oil lifted. They promote small and risky ventures with a low probability of commercial success using *production sharing* and *risk service* agreements. Successful efforts are rewarded in kind with crude oil or from the proceeds derived from the sale of crude oil. Under these arrangements the company bears the risk for the privilege of exploiting potential reserves. Most oil comes from the more prolific fields that are exploited using straight *service contracts*. The Aramco service contract with Saudi Arabia, for example, calls for a fifteen cent service fee for each barrel lifted. The ENOCs generally receive a percentage share of oil lifted in their respective countries. In addition to these contractual arrangements, there is a complex array of agreements and joint ventures among the majors, independents, INOCs, and ENOCs.

The net result of these contractual relations is that each participant is entitled to a quantity of crude oil. In most cases, they can calculate, or at least estimate, original acquisition costs. These may vary from one or two dollars to several hundred dollars per tonne, depending on the market participant. Almost regardless of acquisition costs, the group holding title to the crude seeks the highest possible price within the context of individually proscribed marketing prodcedures. Owing to the sheer volume involved and the necessity for continuous operations, almost all crude oil is originally sold on a long-term contractual basis. Spot transactions and state trading are the exceptions, but do occur among ENOCs, INOCs, the independents, and in resale markets. The volume of spot trading is estimated at 5 to 15 percent of crude-oil transactions, but the estimates at the higher end of this range involve double counting.

Complex Interactions. There is some confusion about who determines contract prices and the level of output. In general, sellers can determine either output or prices but not both. In essence, the member countries of OPEC, and especially Saudi Arabia, determine the overall level of the Saudi marker-crude price. Each producer establishes the prices of its own crudes with the result that there are differentials around the marker-crude price. Given these prices, it is the ultimate consumers who determine the overall volume taken. The international majors, INOCs, and independents serve as intermediaries and determine from whom they will buy. These companies exert little influence on the overall level of production except in their role as producers on their own account; similarly, they have little influence on prices.

The decision of the intermediary companies to buy from one producer rather than another is based to a large extent on relative prices. Naturally, many companies are constrained by long-term contractual arrangements from switching their source of supply. Marginal adjustments, however, are possible and do occur. Market share of the individual producing-countries often swing widely during a three to four year period, varying by as much as 30 percent from average values. Thus, production has ranged from 40 to 100 percent of capacity in several OPEC member countries in recent years. It is the selected price differentials that largely determine these levels of capacity utilization.

The Importance of Size and Market Shares

The importance of size to the probable development of crude-oil futures trading cannot be overemphasized. In general, large entities are self-insuring and need not use futures markets for hedging. On the other hand, large enterprises are frequently so visible that they cannot effectively speculate. The aspects of size considered are production by major country and company, as well as refinery capacity by company. Market shares in these areas will strongly influence the volume of crude-oil futures trading, since the larger exporting countries and international majors, although potentially the largest short hedgers, will be the last to utilize the futures market.

Crude Production by Country

The four largest oil-producing countries in the non-Communist world in 1980 were Saudi Arabia, the United States, Iraq, and Venezuela, which together account for over one-half of total non-Communist output. The top eight countries produced 68 percent and the top fourteen produced 87 percent of the total. Ten of these countries are member countries of OPEC, which, along with Mexico, have centralized control over the production and dispostiion of their crude oil. The United Kingdom, Canada, and the United States round out the list; their systems are far more decentralized.

The producing countries with centralized administration rarely sell on spot markets even when spot prices are double those received on a long-term contractual basis. Many important officials view the spot market as the playground for speculators and have written resale restrictions into their long-term contracts to prevent buyers from dealing with third parties. While the purpose of resale restrictions is partly political, they nevertheless impede spot-market trade.

Crude Production by Company

The international majors produce more than half of the oil flowing from noncommunist countries. They dispose of most of their share of production through their own refineries and marketing channels, including sales to INOCs and independent refiners. They also sell oil among themselves. The majors, however, are not net sellers of crude. On the contrary, these firms are net buyers of crude, as they often must repurchase from ENOCs some of the latter's share of production.

The majors do not constitute a homogeneous group. Exxon has long enjoyed nearly equal downstream and upstream involvement and about equal strength in the U.S. and European markets. Shell and Mobil have traditionally been crude-short or net buyers, whereas Socal and Texaco have been long on crude by virtue of their ownership of Aramco. Gulf's situation is similar to that of Texaco and SoCal, but much weaker; Gulf derived its claim as a major from its joint-concession in Kuwait with BP. Gulf's Kuwaiti position, however, has been seriously eroded. BP became crude-short by virtue of the Iranian nationalization in 1951 and the formation of the Iranian National Oil Company. BP has important stakes in Alaska and in the North Sea, however, and once again has a more balanced operation. Naturally, BP and Shell have a relatively strong refining and marketing position in Europe, whereas Mobil, SoCal, Texaco, and Gulf have relatively greater strength in the United States. Again, Exxon is highly integrated and strong vertically and horizontally in most markets.

The independents, considered as a group, are crude-short, especially the European companies, which are relatively small and confined mostly to refining and marketing in Europe. The principal INOCs include ENI, VEBA, Cie Francaise des Petroles (CFP) and S.N. Elf Aquitaine (SNEA). They are generally larger than the European independents, about equal in size to the larger American independents, but small compared to the international majors. The INOCs and independents are very much alike except for their form of ownership and control. They are involved in most phases of petroleum operations but are particularly important in refining and marketing. These are highly competitive sectors linked to the not-so-competitive producing sector that is dominated by the ENOCs and exporting-country bureaucracies. Most independents and INOCs have little geographical diversification and insufficient direct access to crude oil bought on long-term contract. They are the most vulnerable to price variations. An assessment of these production market-shares with respect to the potential for futures trading will be made in conjunction with refinery concentration.

Refining Capacity

Refining capacity is highly concentrated in the hands of the international majors, but they are gradually yielding market-shares to the ENOCs, INOCs, and independents. In 1970, the majors controlled 55.4 percent of refinery capacity worldwide. They were strongest in Europe and weakest in North America (see table 13–1). Their position has deteriorated outside the North American and European markets, but they remain strong almost everywhere.

Crude-Oil Futures: Louisiana Light

Crude-oil futures have frequently been hailed as necessary and inevitable responses to the vagaries of the market. Just as often, however, crude-oil trading has been shrugged off as impractical because of a host of obstacles, ranging from politial differences, to an insufficient number of principal traders, to intractable problems of quality differentials.

Swimming upstream, in late 1981, the Chicago Board of Trade proposed a crude-futures contract. The Louisiana light *sweet* contract was expected to start in May/June 1982. Based on Louisiana light, the contract permits delivery of fifteen foreign crudes, all within the range of API gravities 35°–40°. Most of the deliverable foreign crudes would trade at a slight premium. The contract (see appendix H) provides for quality differentials of two cents per barrel per degree. Delivery can be by pipeline or tanker at selected Gulf ports in Louisiana.

The CBT's initiative in introducing a crude-oil contract caught many analysts by surprise. There have been some suggestions that the CBT was trying to get a jump on NYMEX, which dominates the U.S. oil-futures trade, on crude trading. CBT has proposed a number of Gulf Coast contracts, including No. 2 and gasoline, and seems to be attempting to carve a permanent niche for itself in the petroleum trade.

While CBT spokespeople and some commodity analysts feel that the time is ripe to commence a futures trade in crude, NYMEX representatives and oil industry people have expressed scepticism; IPE staff members also have voiced their doubts. The critics point to a number of problems they expect will stifle the development of the crude-oil futures trade. First, acceptable crudes must be defined. Different crudes, moreover, must be readily identifiable upon delivery. Even if quality differences are resolvable for most buyers and sellers, certain crude slates may not be acceptable to refiners. Depending upon refinery configurations and the product demands (that is, gasoline and gas oil), different quality crudes may not be usable. Second, if large volumes of crude are traded, as is traditionally the case on world oil markets, there may be major problems of logistics and storage. Moreover, the Louisiana sweet contract provides for delivery through a system of warehouse receipts, an approach that is unfamiliar to most oil traders. Third, doubts stem from the highly politicized atmosphere surrounding crude oil. To a far greater degree than refined petroleum products, crude is prone to political controls and uses. This is true on international as well as national markets. The extent of government involvement in crude-oil markets might interfere with or even prohibit the smooth workings of a futures trade in crude.

Potential For Crude-Oil Futures Trading

Size of Market

Since crude oil is the single most important commodity traded, as measured by market value, it obviously has the potential to become the largest of all futures markets. In the more highly developed markets, such as wheat, the underlying value of actuals and futures contracts exhibits a ratio of about 1:1. If this ratio were to hold for crude oil, annual trading volume would be 24 million (100 tonne) contracts. This would make crude oil the clear volume leader. Trading volume on the order of one tenth that amount would be impressive.

Potential Market Participants

The small refiners and independent oil companies are more vulnerable to the risks associated with price variability than the international majors, INOCs, ENOCs, and other oil exporting-country bureaucracies. The largest exporting countries with centralized control of crude-oil production and distribution are the least vulnerable to price variations, but they do experience variations in output and total revenue. They are not likely to engage in futures trading, however, since they do not even use spot markets very extensively and, in fact, are intolerant of them. On the other hand, some ENOCs, including the Iranian National Oil Company and Soviet-state traders, have utilized the spot market when prices seemed particularly advantageous. The producing countries could benefit from a well developed crude-oil futures market by selling short when spot and futures greatly exceed contract prices. Thus, although the producing countries are likely to be among the last to engage in futures trading, there is a possibility they will participate once the advantages are perceived. Thereafter, trading may increase at a rapid pace. Alternatively, crude-oil futures may pose a threat to the cohesion of OPEC, or be perceived as a threat, as will be explained in the following section. In any case, the possibility of extensive involvement during the 1980s seems remote.

The INOCs and international majors are somewhat better candidates for trading crude-oil futures. Since they do engage in some spot trading at present, it is logical that they might participate to a modest extent in futures trading. If they were to hedge even one barrel in ten on futures, it would constitute about five percent of world trade or over 2 million contracts annually. Involvement at that level is a distinct possibility by the late 1980s, provided that certain technical difficulties related to contract specifications can be worked out.

The independents and small refiners are prime candidates for trading crude-oil futures since they are short sellers of refined products and would be short to a greater extent if they could go long in crude-oil futures (unless they choose to hedge these). The main hurdles to their use of the futures market pertain to the acceptability of technical specifications of the crude and to its deliverability. If these difficulties can be overcome futures trading in crude oil could become very large.

Technical Obstacles

The primary technical obstacle to crude-oil futures trading lies in the lack of homogeneity in the product. Crude oil varies in quality in its natural state from a liquid of high viscosity that will barely pour to almost pure gasoline. All oils are lighter than water at normal temperature and pressure and have a specific gravity less than 1.0. The very lightest crudes have a specific gravity of about .78, whereas crudes with a specific gravity greater than .93 are considered heavy. Most crudes produced at present fall in the .85 to .89 specific-gravity range. In addition, crude oils have varying levels of impurities such as sulphur and vanadium. Crudes that have high concentrations of impurities have a pungent sulphur odor and are appropriately called sour. Sweet crudes are low in sulphur content, require less refinery processing and, therefore, command a higher price.

Qualitative differences affect the value of specific crudes and may even make them unacceptable for delivery to certain refineries. If the market values assigned to the quality differentials were small and relatively stable, delivery of lower (higher) quality crudes could be accepted at proscribed discounts (premiums). The substantial price differentials based on quality, however, are inherently unstable because they depend on the weather, business conditions, and a variety of other factors related to availability of specific crudes. A method must be worked out to establish appropriate price differentials for crude-oil futures trading to become widely adopted.

One alternative would be to eliminate deliverability altogether and allow a panel of experts to specify a settlement price each day in the delivery month. On the final delivery day the announced settlement price would be binding. There are, however, legal obstacles in most countries. The function of futures trading as a risk-management tool is not sufficiently understood by political leaders, so they generally insist that commodities be deliverable under the terms of a futures contract. An alternative that might prove acceptable would be to retain delivery but allow a panel of experts to specify appropriate discounts or penalties for delivery of lower quality crudes. The object should be, however, to construct a futures market in which delivery is rare.

Practical obstacles may be even more insurmountable than legal and political problems. No futures contracts have ever been traded on the basis proposed. Although futures markets are marginal suppliers of commodities, they must retain their ability to provide quality product to remain effective. Because futures are risk-minimizing tools, trader needs to know the standards of the product backing the contract. He will not want to wait for a judgment by experts establishing the value of what he has already purchased.

Conclusion

Prior to the success of OPEC in limiting output and raising oil prices there was little risk associated with price variability. The evolving market-structure, however, has exposed a large and growing segment of the industry. The degree of exposure varies from the relatively secure position of the ENOCs to that of non-integrated small refiners that buy mostly on the spot market. The international majors, INOCs and partially integrated independents occupy the middle ground. This complex and changing market-structure bodes well for trading crude-oil futures contracts.

There are technical impediments related to the homogeneity of products and their deliverability, but these do not appear insolvable in the long run. The history of other commodity markets shows that the time required to proceed from spot to forward, or from forward to futures trading, is relatively short. Precisely when the market structure will become sufficiently competitive and when the technical impediments to futures trading will be worked out is subject to speculation. It would not be too surprising, however, if crude-oil futures were traded extensively by the early 1990s.

Table 13–1
World and Regional Refinery Capacity and Distribution

Refiner	Million Barrels per Day Refinery Capacity		Percentage Share	
	1970	1975	1970	1975
Total World				
Majors	23.95	29.46	55.4	49.8
ENOCs	0.71	1.88	1.6	3.2
INOCs and independents	18.55	27.81	42.9	47.0
Total	43.21	59.15	100.0	100.0
North America				
Majors	6.83	7.90	48.8	46.3
ENOCs	0	0	0	0
INOCs and independents	7.18	9.15	51.2	53.7
Total	14.01	17.05	100.0	100.0
Europe				
Majors	9.45	11.86	63.7	58.0
ENOCs	0	0	0	0
INOCs and independents	5.38	8.58	36.3	42.0
Total	14.83	20.44	100.0	100.0
Other				
Majors	7.67	9.70	53.4	44.8
ENOCs	0.71	1.88	4.9	8.7
INOCs and independents	5.99	10.08	41.7	46.5
Total	14.37	21.66	100.0	100.0

Source: U.S. Department of Energy, *Technical Analysis of the International Petroleum Market,* June 1978, pp. 257–263.

Table 13-2
World and Regional Crude-Oil Production and Distribution

Producer	Million Barrels per Day Production		Percentage Share	
	1970	1975	1970	1975
Total World				
Majors	25.55	24.84	64.0	56.5
ENOCs	0.82	5.45	2.0	12.4
INOCs and independents	13.56	13.69	34.0	31.1
Total	39.93	43.98	100.0	100.0
North America				
Majors	5.17	4.81	40.5	41.0
ENOCs	0	0	0	0
INOCs and independents	7.61	6.92	59.5	59.0
Total	12.78	11.73	100.0	100.0
Europe				
Majors	0.21	0.19	47.7	31.1
ENOCs	0	0	0	0
INOCs and independents	0.23	0.42	52.3	68.9
Total	0.44	0.61	100.0	100.0
Other				
Majors	20.17	19.84	75.5	62.7
ENOCs	0.82	5.45	3.1	17.2
INOCs and independents	5.72	6.35	21.4	20.2
Total	26.71	31.64	100.0	100.0

Source: U.S. Department of Energy, *Technical Analyses of The International Petroleum Market,* June 1978, pp. 257-263.

14

Petroleum Futures and Industry Performance

Albert L. Danielsen

The impact of futures trading on industry structure and performance depends on the existing structure. The recent performance, and the course of futures trading itself. Structure and performance can be comprehended without too much difficulty, petroleum-futures markets are insufficiently developed and the extent of their use by hedgers is too limited to make it possible to predict with certainty what course futures trading will follow. A primary task of this chapter is to explain the present structure of the industry and to evaluate its recent performance. The potential impact of petroleum futures will be evaluated under the assumption that trading in futures continues to develop in both crude oil and refined products.

Present Market Structure

The structure of international petroleum markets is neither purely competitive nor fully monopolized. Relatively cooperative relations are obvious in crude-oil production, whereas more competitive arrangements predominate in the tanker, refinery, and marketing segments of the industry. Overlaying these sectors are country-specific trade restrictions, such as tariffs and quotas, nationalistic ownership requirements, preferential shipping regulations, restrictive resale agreements, and an almost endless array of taxes on production, distribution, and consumption.

Reserves and Production

OPEC is the central organization promoting cooperation among the producing countries, but it is little more than a forum for the expression of views among its principal participants. Saudi Arabia has the largest reserves and is, therefore, the most important and influential oil exporting country in the world. Iran and Kuwait have combined reserves nearly equal to those of Saudi Arabia. Iraq, the United Arab Emirates (UAE), Venezuela, Nigeria, Libya, and Qatar are the other large OPEC producers, and each has reserves in excess of 3 billion tonnes. These countries have about two-thirds of the world's liquid petroleum reserves and produce almost one-half of total world output. They are clearly the dominant

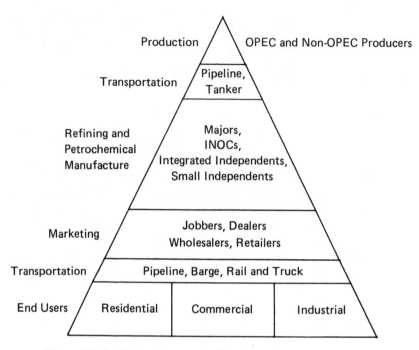

Figure 14-1. Market Structure of the Petroleum Industry

group in world petroleum markets and are likely to remain so well into the twenty-first century. In fact, Saudi Arabia will more than likely produce oil in the twenty-second century.

The only countries with potential reserves on the order of the OPEC members are the Soviet Union, Mexico, the United States, China, the United Kingdom and Canada. These producers may be regarded as a competitive fringe around the OPEC cartel. They are able to market their oil at prices comparable to those received by members of OPEC. Probable reserves in other countries are much smaller. Large revenues above production costs are the general rule for all concerned. These net revenues are taxed to varying degrees by competitive-fringe and minor-producer governments.

Refining and Marketing

Market structures are extraordinarily complex downstream from crude-oil production. Oil touches almost everyone, so there are millions of participants in the market process. Figure 14-1 is an abstract view of the overall market structure. Residential consumers as well as commercial and industrial enterprises are the

end-users of a variety of refined products and petrochemicals. Some of the industrial users are larger than the international majors themselves (as measured by
assets, value added, and so on). Others are individual proprietorships or private
individuals. There are a wide variety of contractual relations and exposures to
risk associated with price variability among these market participants.

Higher up the distribution chain are the petroleum retailers, wholesalers,
dealers, and jobbers, they are interrelated and draw upon the products of refiners and petrochemical manufacturers. Both refining and marketing are highly
competitive industries. Naturally, there are more enterprises engaged in marketing than in refining, but even the refining industry has a very large number of
firms. Entry or expansion is realtively easy, not withstanding environmental
regulations that have made it more complicated to complete specific projects.
Worldwide refining capacity is over 11 million tonnes per day, or about one-
third more than refinery throughput. This excess capacity has come about
through a combination of the ease of entry, the decline in world oil demand
since 1979, and the long lead times in completing refinery reconstruction to
reduce the capacity surpluses.

Refiners are, in turn, connected to the crude-oil producers through a variety
of long-term and spot contractual relations. There is a network of pipelines,
tankers, barges, rail cars, trucks, and storage facilities used to deliver and store
products at each level of the distribution chain. In general, the transport sector
is either highly competitive or regulated by the state. The international tanker
market is a competitive industry, whereas most pipelines are subject to rate-of-
return regulations.

Recent Market Performance

Market performance refers to the relation between prices and costs, as well as to
variability of prices. In general, crude-oil and refined-product prices move in the
same direction, but they do not necessarily move by the same magnitude. Refined-product prices often vary when crude prices are stable. Crude-oil prices
largely determine the major swings in refined-product prices, but some variations
are due to seasonal and cyclical forces.

Crude-Oil Pricing

Most crude oil is initially traded in what is essentially a *basing point* pricing
system, with the Arabian Gulf as the base point. The system evolved during the
late 1960s and early 1970s because the Arabian Gulf became the leading oil-
exporting center. The system works because the leading oil-exporting countries
are willing to expand and contract output to meet demand at specified contract

prices. These exporting countries serve as residual suppliers in much the same way that the international majors did during the 1950s.

As currently constituted, crude oil bought on long-term contract is subject to price change without notice. The official price is simply the price specified by the exporting country on the date a tanker arrives at the loading port. If prices are changed while loading, that portion loaded after the price increase goes into effect is billed at the higher price. Contract prices tend to remain stable for prolonged periods, but may be adjusted frequently when markets are disorderly. Spot prices fluctuate because each tanker or barge lot is subject to negotiation.

The refiner's choice of one crude over another depends upon his geographic location, refinery equipment, regulatory environment, and expected product prices. In general, the refiner buys lower priced crudes if quality and transport costs are identical. He is willing to pay a premium for crudes with a low specific gravity and low sulphur content. When price differentials are sufficiently great, the refiner buys crudes he regards as undervalued. Thus, sellers determine prices, but buyers determine volume and market shares among suppliers. Sellers can and do influence volume and their own market share by selecting differentials that are attractive to buyers.

Demand Patterns

The volume of oil traded varies within fairly narrow limits. A year-to-date increase or reduction on the order of 5 percent is unusual, but swings of this magnitude do occur. The primary reasons for demand variations are seasonal and cyclical patterns of consumption and inventory buildups or drawdowns. On rare occasions these reinforce one another.

Seasonal demand variations are dominated by gas-oil consumption because this product is used by residential, commercial, and industrial users for space heating. Gasoline exhibits an opposite seasonal pattern, but heating oil constitutes a larger fraction of OECD refinery output and dominates the seasonal demand pattern. The magnitude of these seasonal demand variations is on the order of one-half million tonnes per day in the International Energy Agency (IEA) countries. Such demand variations are generally handled by utilizing storage capacity, which is a less costly alternative than maintaining excess production, transport, and refinery capacity. Thus, seasonal inventory buildups and drawdowns of refined products are normal. Unusually cold or warm winters, or conditions that prolong vacation driving seasons cause inordinate demands on the system and result in moderate price variations.

Demand variations associated with the business cycle cannot be anticipated with as much certainty as those associated with seasonal variations. Industrial, commercial, and transport enterprises use less energy when operating at less than full capacity and these cyclical swings can be quite pronounced. On a world scale, cyclical demand variations have caused OPEC production to vary by over one-half million tonnes per day. These are in addition to seasonal demand variations.

The influence of inventory buildups and drawdowns on overall demand is very imperfectly understood. The demand for oil consists of purchases for immediate consumption and purchases for stockpiling. Since it is costly to hold large stockpiles, oil companies build inventories when they anticipate rising prices, thus increasing the demand for oil and driving actual prices higher. At $250 per tonne and a 20 percent interest rate, the annual financial cost of holding a tonne of inventories is $50 plus storage costs. Thus, refiners do not hold many tonnes in excess of current requirements when they anticipate stable or declining prices.

The oil companies have anticipated major swings in oil prices to a very limited extent. Inventories were built during 1973-1974 when prices were rising. Inventories are always increased prior to OPEC ministerial meetings when price increases are anticipated. Inventories were built substantially during 1979. On the other hand, inventories were drawn down in 1975-1976, 1978, and 1980-1981 when spot prices were stable or declining. A reasonable assessment of company behavior is that they have sought short-term profit-maximization goals and have not anticipated major price movements by more than one or two months.

Taking into account the cyclical and seasonal variations in consumption and inventory changes, OPEC production has varied by well over 1 million tonnes per day, or by 25 percent of capacity. If OPEC did not have the ability to expand and contract output over such a wide range, price variations would be more severe than those that have been observed. It is the ability to shut-in capacity and develop reserves slowly that has enabled OPEC to maintain contract prices during periods of slack demand.

Spot and Contract Prices

The dramatic price increases that occurred during the 1970s were associated with the 1973-1974 Arab oil embargo and the Iranian revolution in 1979. Between these two periods contract and spot prices were relatively stable. Spot and contract prices are related to each other, and inventories played an important role in elevating prices. During both 1973 and 1979, spot prices led contract prices upward and reached new peaks. Similarly, inventories were accumulated in 1973 and 1979 as prices moved upward. These inventory buildups drove spot prices higher than they would otherwise have gone and encouraged OPEC members to raise contract prices. Competitive, fringe producers naturally followed suit, and there ensued an upward spiral of spot prices, inventory accumulations, and contract prices. After the speculative fever subsided and the industrial recessions of 1975 and 1980 got well under way, OPEC members cut production in an effort to maintain contract prices. Spot prices fell to the level of contract prices and below.

Forward Delivery and Futures Markets

Dealing in physical commodities exposes business firms to risk associated with price variations, but insurance principles do not apply because all dealers at a given level of the distribution chain are exposed to similar risks. The possibility of organizing a futures market arises from the fact that there are gains and losses among the various market participants. A rise in price confers gains on those holding the commodity, whereas those who wish to purchase are losers. Similarly, a decline in price imposes a loss on those holding the commodity, whereas prospective buyers gain. Dealers seeking price protection, or hedged positions, could balance long commitments in the commodity itself with short sales for forward delivery. Thus, it is theoretically possible to hedge through forward contracting alone, but it is costly to devise offsetting transactions.

In general, futures markets provide the opportunity to tailor more precisely hedged positions and to extend them farther into the future. They allow market participants to rationalize inherently risky forward commitments and, thus, remove the element of gambling from business transactions. Futures markets also allow the expression of opinions about equilibrium prices by those outside the trade—that is, by speculators. By their very nature, futures markets are more competitive than forward markets are alone.

Hedging without Futures Markets

Forward delivery commitments are essentially uncovered short positions, whereas forward commitments to take delivery are uncovered longs. Without futures contracts a refiner *may* be able to balance commitments to deliver refined products with commitments to take delivery of crude oil. Similarly, a firm marketing refined products *may* be able to hedge commitments by arranging offsetting contractual obligations with a refiner and commercial user. A company integrated from wellhead to pump inherently hedges over a wide range of activities. A non-integrated enterprise must carefully plan and coordinate both acquisition and disposition of the commodity to accomplish the same objectives.

In general, it is not possible for a non-integrated enterprise to fully offset commitments through forward contracting because contractual relations are not identical in the acquisition and disposition phases of their operations. Thus, an industrial user may operate on an annual budget and seek full-year commitments for residual fuel oil. Wholesalers may have access to resid for only one month and refiners access to crude oil at firm fixed-prices for only two months. Beyond those periods they are exposed to risks associated with new inventory acquisitions. Under these conditions the industrial user, wholesaler, refiner, or any combination of the three will have to bear the risk associated with adverse price movements. In addition, hedging through forward markets alone is difficult because trading generally involves physical delivery and a matching of particular qualities, quantities, and delivery dates.

The Futures Overlay

The primary function of futures markets is to reduce risk through hedging. Delivery can be more precisely offset with termination of a futures contract than with a forward commitment. The problems associated with quantity and quality are standardized even if they are not fully resolved. Empirical studies have revealed that the success of hedging in reducing risk varies directly with the magnitude of spot-price changes. Thus, the cover provided by hedging is most effective in those contracts where it is most needed.

Speculators play a well known and important role in futures markets. They are essentially middlemen who provide a form of insurance against the risk of price fluctuations. The nature of this involvement increases liquidity and lowers average transactions costs. Beyond these laudable functions, it is often claimed that speculators reduce price variations by buying when prices are low and selling when they are high, but empirical proof substantiating such claims is lacking. Proponents of this view argue that speculators aim to make profits and to do so they must buy cheap and sell dear. This implies that speculators are better informed than dealers, a view which seems contrary to the facts, since it is well known that most small speculators lose their shirts before abandoning futures trading. Large speculators seem to fare better.

In a similar vein, futures have been proclaimed to play a role in guiding production and inventory decisions, thereby stabilizing prices and industry revenue. Some of these claims are little more than wishful thinking or rationalizations in favor of expanding futures trading. Others may apply to one market, during a particular time period, but may not be applicable to commodity markets generally. A central issue is whether futures prices represent forecasts of cash prices. If they do, then there are good reasons to believe that futures trading will have a stabilizing influence on the variables in question; otherwise, there are none.

In fact, there is no basis whatsoever for the claim that futures prices represent a forecast of cash prices. A new and profound influence, such as the Iran-Iraq War in 1980, affects spot and all futures prices to about the same extent. Spot and futures prices, should, therefore, be regarded as forecasts of future cash prices to about the same degree. It is best to think of spot and futures prices as a constellation of prices moving in response to the same basic forces. Based on considerations such as these, Tomek and Gray have stated the issue succinctly:

The existence of a convenient institutional arrangement (i.e., futures markets) for introducing a temporal dimension into price undoubtedly extends the price-making horizon and refines the assessment of the time utility of a commodity. But, at least in circumstances involving continuous inventories, forecasts are reflected just as much in cash and nearby futures as in distant futures prices. *The element of expectations is imparted to the whole temporal constellation of price quotations, and futures prices reflect essentially no prophecy that is not reflected in the cash price and is in that sense already fulfilled.*[1]

Effects on Industry Structure

Futures trading may be expected to marginally affect industry structure at all levels of the distribution chain. The most immediate effects will occur downstream in refining and marketing, but the most important ones may be upstream through their influence on OPEC. In general, these changes will make petroleum markets more competitive.

Futures Trading in Refined Products

Users of refined products can insulate themselves against price increases by going long in futures, whereas refiners can lock in a profit by selling short. Small firms can benefit from such transactions because banks and other financial institutions are willing to finance a relatively large proportion of hedged positions. Thus, small firms will be able to command more resources to compete against larger enterprises. This assumes a contango sufficient to ensure a normal business profit from a fully hedged strategy. Otherwise, the use of petroleum futures will not become widespread.

Futures trading in refined products will permit companies with ownership rights in crude oil to capture carrying charges by promising delivery far into the future. Thus, the equilibrium contango in a well developed petroleum-futures market will fall short of storage costs. The ratio of contango to storage costs may be expected to vary inversely with the delivery month. Thus, futures will promote greater competition in marketing and distribution and erode profit margins for those not involved in futures trading. The majors and ENOCs could gain substantially by early entry into futures as short sellers. They will be net losers in the long term, however, because futures will make these markets more competitive. The majors and ENOCs may be expected to suffer most, whereas relative gains for the smaller independents may be anticipated.

Futures Trading in Crude Oil

Futures trading in crude oil will permit non-integrated producers to capture carrying charges further upstream by promising delivery farther into the future. The effects on contango in relation to storage costs and upon competition will be similar to those specified for refined products. This could pose a threat to the stability of OPEC because it opens a new avenue of competition for those within the cartel who may be willing to take advantage of the opportunity. The most probable outcome, however, is that the smaller OPEC producers will establish relations with dealers to sell short in futures when markets are weak, thus exerting additional pressure on the constellation of futures and spot prices.

Futures trading could strengthen the position of OPEC if large producers become active and the member countries devise a cooperative rather than competitive futures strategy. For example, short selling could become so extensive that futures prices would be characterized by a small contango or backwardation. This would reduce the incentive to hold commercial stocks and would reduce delivery costs. The system would be similar to that of the 1960s, except that the bureaucracies of OPEC members and ENOCs, rather than the integrated majors, would be in control. In fact, almost any of the larger countries could exert an important influence on carrying charges and market structure. It is not possible to predict the precise path that will develop.

Effects on Industry Performance

Futures trading will affect the level and variability of spot and contract prices but the magnitude and direction of the effects are problematic. These will depend on market structure, and particularly upon the extent of involvement on the short or long side of the market.

The price level and variability are interrelated since OPEC members are willing to cut production to maintain prices. If long hedgers predominate, the contango will equal storage costs and greater inventories will be held outside OPEC. This will increase average distribution-costs but could stabilize the price level. Large inventories are not sufficient in themselves, however, to guarantee greater price stability, since it is the rate at which inventories are built up or drawn down that determines overall demand and prices. Nevertheless, large inventories held outside OPEC and managed properly have the potential to stabilize prices.

If short hedgers predominate in futures trading, the contango will be small and there will be few incentives to hold inventories outside OPEC. This will lower average storage-costs but could make prices subject to greater variability, thus contributing to sharp periodic upward price movements. The oil stockpiling policies of consuming countries could override market-induced incentives to hold inventories and, thus, alter the level and variability of prices. There is insufficient information about the course futures trading and inventory policy will follow to be dogmatic.

Conclusion

Futures trading will affect both the structure and performance of the petroleum industry. The primary effects will be to make the industry more competitive and strengthen the independents at the expense of the majors. OPEC will be affected, but futures trading could either weaken or strengthen its position. Similarly, the effects of futures on price variability and level will probably be small, but the marginal effects could either moderate or exacerbate price variability and either raise or lower prices. If these statements appear more hedged than speculative, then they are probably on the mark. The outcome depends on interactive policies of individual market participants and is, therefore, problematic.

Note

1. William G. Tomek and Roger W. Gray, "Temporal Relationships Among Prices on Commodity Futures Markets," in A.E. Peck ed., *Selected Writings on Futures Markets,* Vol II. (Chicago: Board of Trade of the City of Chicago, 1977), p. 139.

15 Government Petroleum Stockpiling

The Logic of Stockpiling

The stockpiling of crude and oil products by governments, government agencies, and industry (under the direction of government or for commercial reasons) is a major fact of life in oil markets. Sizes of company and country stocks, as well as additions to and sales from those stocks, must be carefully watched by participants in the oil industry. The volumes involved are large, and changes in stockpiles can have significant effects on supplies and prices.

The idea of stockpiling is based upon one basic assumption: it is better to bear the cost of developing and maintaining a stockpile than it is to risk a shortage. The rationale is similar to that employed in futures markets with respect to supply and price. In the most general sense, if it is more costly to assume the risks of a supply interruption and shortfall than it is to hold reserves, petroleum should be stockpiled. Although risks and costs are traditionally expressed in economic terms, political and social issues also are important to decisions on petroleum stockpiling.

As energy-intensive nations whose economies are heavily dependent on petroleum, the Western countries would be badly hurt by an oil supply shortfall if they had no strategic stocks. Without available substitutes or stocks, a petroleum supply interruption could mean economic havoc for the OECD states. Strategically, a shortage would severely restrict military preparedness. Politically, a state would be ransom to countries wielding oil power; domestically the government would be subject to various interest-group pressures. Socially, a significant or prolonged petroleum shortfall would mean reduced states of consumption, lowered standards of living, and a lengthy period of social readjustment. Measured against the risks—which, in the extreme, might spell military defeat, or economic collapse—the cost of stockpiling petroleum is relatively inexpensive insurance.

Insurance policy aspects aside, the actual costs of stockpiling petroleum are significant: properly designed facilities must be built and set aside, the oil must be bought and paid for, and tank farms and distribution systems have to be maintained. Construction of stockpile storage facilities already has cost the OECD states tens-of-billions of dollars, at a unit cost ranging from $1 to $10 per barrel of capacity. The investment required, moreover, is a sunken cost that does not yield any economic return. The value of petroleum stocks will most likely appreciate (although that is not guaranteed) and any surplus sales may be made at prices higher than acquisition costs. As stockpile sales would be used only under certain supply conditions and depleted stocks must always be replaced if the stockpile is to remain useful, stockpiles are a big net-cost item.

In the event of a petroleum supply shortfall, a country has five defensive alternatives:

increase purchases from other sources abroad,

reduce domestic consumption,

draw down stocks,

increase domestic crude-oil production, or

employ alternative forms of energy.

The ability to use some of these strategies depends on circumstances. While diversifying foreign sources of crude is a logical response, this might not be possible under prevailing market conditions. If a producers' embargo is levied or production cutbacks are implemented, sufficient alternative supplies might not exist. IEA members, moreover, are obligated to share any imports equally in the event of a general supply crisis and are pledged not to pursue bilateral deals.

Reducing domestic consumption without suffering adverse affects is an inherently limited alternative. Even the demand restraint envisioned by the IEA scenarios (that is, 7 percent or 10 percent) could not be accomplished without harmful economic consequences. Even a small forced decline in consumption will translate into gross national product (GNP) losses totalling billions of dollars.

Except for those countries that have extensive shut-in capacity, expanding domestic output is not feasible in the short term. The substitution of alternative types of energy is limited by the resources of each country and the special characteristics of petroleum that make it difficult to replace.

Obviously, the usefulness of employing stocks is dependent on the existence of a sufficiently large stockpile. Effective use of a stockpile, however, gives a state increased flexibility in managing its energy supply/demand balance and in coping with supply interruptions. For the IEA states as a whole, petroleum stockpiling is one of the best means of minimizing the negative impacts of a significant supply shortfall. A stockpile equal to ninety days of imports means that a country could survive a 25 percent cut in imports for a full year without curbing consumption. (This assumes that all stocks are available for use in an emergency. In effect, a certain percentage of supplies would not be available.) If a country reduced demand by 10 percent (as the more severe general crisis guidelines of the IEA requires), a ninety-day stockpile would, in theory, permit that country to withstand a 25 percent drop in imports for five years.

Petroleum Stockpiles and the Market

Stockpiles can be economic or strategic. Economic or buffer stocks are used to minimize price fluctuations and the consequences of supply/demand imbalances. Strategic or emergency stocks are used to redress supply shortfalls. IEA mandated oil stocks are for strictly strategic purposes and are not to be used as buffers. Depending upon state policy, stocks might be held by the government or private companies. Oil companies also have commercial stocks to run their own operations. Strategic reserves can be held separate from or combined with commercial stocks, or both.

Private- and public-sector stockpiles of both crude oil and refined products are essential elements in the petroleum supply chain. Industry people are familiar with the seasonal changes in stocks held by the large oil companies, especially by refiners and distributors. Strategic stocks are less well understood. Since volumes held for strategic purposes, often mandated by law, are partially insulated from the logic of the market, their effect upon market behavior is difficult to predict.

Falling prices imperil the value of commercial stocks. Companies and refineries holding stocks are wise to go short in such a market, trying to hedge the value of inventories against a further decline in price. As strategic stockpiles are not justified in terms of commercial judgments, changes in the value of stocks or prices of products may be irrelevant. Because purchases and sales from strategic stocks are political decisions, they may be counter-logical with what might be considered sound market behavior. It is not uncommon for legislatures to refuse to appropriate funds for acquiring supplies when prices are low and to require purchases when prices are high. The absolute sizes of strategic stocks, as well as additions to and sales from those stocks, must be borne in mind by industry traders. While strategic stocks change far less frequently than commercial inventories, in both instances the volumes involved are large, and changes can have significant effects on supply and price.

Petroleum futures-market stocks often are not considered as part of total national supplies. Some analysts have suggested that if carefully documented and rotated, futures-market inventories could be included as a component of total supply in a crisis situation and integrated into national or multinational stockpiling policies. In this respect, NYMEX and CBT stocks are purely American, an attribute exhibited by daily trading patterns and the physical location of stocks. European futures stocks, however, are more ambigious in nationality and sovereignty. IPE gas-oil stocks are located in the Benelux countries, while the market is in London, and traders represent diverse nationalities spanning the European continent and North America. This makes the incorporation of IPE stocks into a general or national stockpiling policy particularly difficult. The diverse parties involved on the IPE could be in conflict if either the United

Kingdom or the Benelux countries sought to treat futures markets as part of a strategic national stockpile. This potential conflict is purely hypothetical. The relationship between futures and strategic stocks has yet to develop and plays no role today in the physical supply/demand picture.

Development of Petroleum Stockpiling

For over eighty years, the industrialized nations have been concerned with assuring a continued and adequate supply of petroleum. Despite periodic scares of impending shortages, supplies remained abundant. Relatively docile Third World oil-producing countries provided the necessary amounts of petroleum for consumption by the West. Traditionally, the largest oil producer in the world, the United States, was a net exporter of petroleum and stood prepared to compensate for any short-term shortages in Europe.

The United States became a net oil importer in 1948. Substantial shut-in capacity, however, meant that the United States still was able to boost production relatively quickly and increase exports in an emergency. The 17 percent and 32 percent increase in U.S. exports in 1956 and 1957, respectively, as a response to the closing of the Suez Canal and associated supply problems in Western Europe, was evidence of this capability.

By the late 1950s, the prospect of the United States providing an emergency source of petroleum was no more. While U.S. petroleum exports in the decade after the war averaged approximately 6 percent of production, by 1960 exports were down to 2.5 percent of domestic output. At the same time, U.S. imports, which averaged less than 12 percent of domestic demand in the immediate postwar period, climbed towards 20 percent. U.S. oil use rose, absorbing increased amounts of world crude and reducing U.S. reserve capacity.

The Suez crisis of 1956 made the European countries painfully aware of their dependency on imported petroleum and the economic and political costs stemming from that dependency. The Organization for European Economic Cooporation (OEEC), forerunner of the OECD, and the petroleum companies managed European supplies allocations during the crisis and successfully minimized the impact of the shortage. In 1958, the OEEC Petroleum Industry Emergency Group (OPEG) was created to coordinate company implementation of OEEC emergency supply requirements. After Suez, the United Kingdom began to develop a reserve petroleum stockpile.

The sense of a united Europe in economic and military affairs seemed to spill over naturally into energy concerns. Beginning with the standards set for the EEC in 1958, the European countries began to adopt a common petroleum-stockpiling policy. In 1954, the Protocol Agreements of Energy for the EEC were signed. Member governments agreed to develop stocks equal to sixty-five days worth of crude imports. In 1968, an EEC directive was issued requiring a sixty-five-day minimum supply. In 1971, the stockpile minimum was increased to ninety days, effective January 1975.

Despite growing imports, the United States remained far less dependent on foreign petroleum than its European and Japanese allies. Within the OECD, energy issues began to receive increased attention. The idea of adopting some type of international sharing and coordination scheme to cope with future supply emergencies was frequently raised by the Europeans. The United States was reluctant to join any sharing plan that might require the export of domestic oil to compensate for a shortfall in Japan or Europe.

The United States favored an emergency plan that dealt only with imports. By reserving domestic production for national consumption and allocating foreign supplies in the event of a crisis, the United States would be far more resilient to supply interruptions than the more import-dependent industrialized states. The United States, moreover, wanted imports from Canada excluded from any import-sharing plan, as these shipments were overland and not by sea routes. U.S. persistence on these issues, as well as other minor squabbles, prevented the formulation of the OECD petroleum emergency allocation system.

The 1973-1974 Arab oil embargo underlined the urgent need for OECD unity. The increased U.S. vulnerability to OPEC proved crucial to the forging of a common OECD stockpiling and emergency allocation plan. U.S. production had peaked in 1970 and began to decline thereafter. By 1973, imports were accounting for more than 35 percent of U.S. oil consumption. The only other major OECD member that was less dependent on oil imports was Canada, which was still a net exporter in 1973. The United Kingdom, France, Germany, Italy, and Japan depended on imports for more than 95 percent of their petroleum consumption. (With the exception of the United Kingdom, these countries are still dependent on imports.)

The Organization of Arab Petroleum Exporting Countries (OAPEC) embargo in 1973-1974 revealed the disarray in OECD policy. The United States, the Netherlands, and Portugal were targets of the embargo. The accompanying production cuts, however, affected all importing nations. The European supply allocation plan was not implemented. Rather, allocation was determined by the major oil companies. The various OECD governments sought to protect themselves by a number of measures, such as arranging bilateral trading (for example, France) and special political relationships with oil producing nations, pressuring domestic-based oil companies to give priority to their respective national markets, and restricting petroleum exports.

Stock drawdowns were employed only sporadically by the OECD states to bridge the supply gap, and none of the major OECD members engaged in a systematic drawdown of crude or product stocks. Drawdowns in one period tended to be compensated for by increases in stocks the next period. When comparing the stocks of the United States, Japan, West Germany, France, Italy and the Netherlands on March 31, 1974, with the levels held on March 31, 1973, a surprising pattern is revealed: in each instance, with the exception of France, crude stocks were the same or higher at the close of the last month of the OAPEC action than they were a year previously, five months before the embargo/cutback. Except for gasoline stocks in West Germany and the Netherlands, gasoline, distillate, and residual-oil stockpiles were unchanged or higher in March 1974 than they were the preceeding March.

It thus seems that all of the OECD states avoided depleting their petroleum stocks. To a large extent, significant drawdowns were avoided because of the short-lived and relatively mild nature of the production reductions. Only the OAPEC countries participated, and then somewhat haphazardly. Some of the non-Arab countries, notably Iran and Nigeria, increased production to gain from the OAPEC cutbacks. Total OPEC production for 1973, moreover, was approximately 15 percent greater than it had been in 1972, and held 1973 levels in 1974. Even during the most severe months of the cutback, November and December of 1973, total OAPEC output was some 6 percent greater than average daily production for the previous year. Continuous stock drawdowns, therefore, were not necessary.

By the time of the Washington Energy Conference in February 1974, OAPEC production was rising toward pre-embargo levels. The trials of the crisis convinced the OECD members that a standby allocation plan and national petroleum stockpile were essential precautions against a repeated, potentially more severe, supply disruption. At the time of the conference, the EEC was implementing a target stockpile level of ninety days of domestic sales, Japan had a goal of sixty days worth of sales, and the United States had no official stockpile requirement.

International Energy Agency Stockpiles

The original terms of the IEA agreement provided for member countries to hold emergency petroleum stocks equal to sixty days of net imports. The reserve requirements were subsequently raised to ninety days of the previous year's imports. Regardless of any subsequent decline in imports, stock levels are not to fall below the required amount based on 1979 import levels. A country with extensive energy output can substitute shut-in domestic production capacity and alternative fuels for up to 15 percent of its stock requirements. IEA stock guidelines are not particularly demanding. EEC stockpile requirements are often higher. The IEA definition of emergency stocks, moreover, is not stringent.

Thus, we can see that crude, products, and unfinished oil count as part of a nation's IEA-mandated stockpile if the supplies are held by consumers as required by law, or they are held in refinery tanks, bulk terminals, pipeline tanks, barges, oil tankers, ports, intercoastal tankers, inland ship bunkers, storage tank bottoms, or working stocks. Excluded as a component of emergency stocks is crude oil yet to be produced, and crude, products, and unfinished oils held in pipelines, rail tank cars, truck tank cars, seagoing ship bunkers, service stations, retail stores, tankers at sea, military stocks, or supplies held by other consumers. Virtually all industry inventories are classified as stocks. The agency assumes correctly that 10 percent of stocks are entrained as tank residues or otherwise unavailable in even the most severe emergency. Total allowable stocks, less 10 percent, count towards a country's emergency stockpile requirements.

Operating and commercial stocks needed for the smooth operation of a large production and distribution network count towards IEA emergency stocks. Minimum working reserves vary for each country, depending on the structure of the domestic industry, including trade flows, distributional networks, and refinery runs. Estimates of minimum working stocks for commercial purposes range from thirty to fifty days of domestic sales. In effect, a country with a ninety-day reserve requirement as defined by the IEA, may actually have only forty to sixty days worth of consumption for use as emergency reserves. The fifty days worth of consumption needed for operating stocks in the United States actually is more than ninety days of net U.S. imports.

Minimum commercial reserve requirements are particularly important in assessing the true availability of emergency petroleum stocks in countries that rely on the private sector to hold stragtegic stocks. Those states that have totally or partially government-held stocks are likely to have a higher share of reserves actually available for use in an emergency than those countries that have strategic stocks combined with commercial inventory stocks.

Under the IEA guidelines, countries with extensive domestic petroleum products, including the United States, the United Kingdom, Norway, and Canada, indicate emergency reserve levels that are inflated. In each of these countries ninety days of imports are less than the minimum reserve levels needed for the operations of the domestic oil industries. Similarly, states that have large refinery industries servicing export markets, such as Italy and the Netherlands, can easily satisfy IEA reserve criteria because refinery stocks are counted as part of IEA emergency stockpiles.

IEA definitions exclude seaborne crude from being counted as part of a nation's emergency reserve. This appears somewhat contradictory, as upon arrival in port these supplies would be virtually 100 percent available in a supply crisis. Then again, tankers can be sunk by enemy action in wartime. At any given time, thirty to forty-five days worth of imports might be in transit on seaborne tankers, depending on market conditions and delivery lead times. These supplies offer importers an increased measure of protection against a supply crisis that is not incorporated into the IEA stockpile/emergency management plan. Re-routing tankers was an important ingredient in company petroleum allocations during the 1973–1974 crisis and would probably play an important role in handling logistical and supply problems in any future crisis.

Although IEA stockpiles are designed for strategic purposes, purchases and sales from stocks cannot be insulated from world prices. Spot-market purchases for stockpiles in 1979—responding to the turn of events in Iran—added to the anxieties created by the disruption of the Iranian oil industry. The buying panic forced prices to record levels. At the Tokyo Economic Summit in June 1979, the industrialized countries agreed to forgo all purchases for stockpiling when such purchases contributed to the upward pressure on prices. A consensus also was reached on mutual consultation about stockpile purchases.

The Iran-Iraq War prompted new fears that a stockpile-buying spree would recur. On October 1, 1980, the IEA urged governments and private companies to avoid undue disturbances to the spot market. Prodded by the IEA, most member states engaged in a paced, orderly stock drawdown to offset the shortfall caused by the war. Careful management of stockpile sales effectively maintained the group drawdown sufficient to balance supply and demand that the IEA governing board had called for at the October session. A similar drawdown for the first quarter of 1981 was implemented.

Currently, every IEA member except Turkey satisfies the ninety-day agency stockpile requirement. The IEA estimated total stocks of the twenty-one members at 3.25 billion barrels (bbls) as of July 1, 1980. This is 4 percent less than estimated stocks of 3.39 billion bbls nine months earlier, indicating a combined stock drawdown of 140 million bbls during this period. Estimated IEA stockpiles for the last three years are:

January 1, 1979 — 3.01 billion bbls.

January 1, 1980 — 3.09 billion bbls.

January 1, 1981 — 3.24 billion bbls.

Softening trends in the world oil market have prompted a number of IEA countries to resume stockpile purchases. Market surpluses and declining prices are allowing countries to acquire supplies on terms that are very favorable compared to those of a year earlier. The agency estimated total stocks were 3.32 billion bbls at October 1981. This required an average monthly rate of acquisition of 8.9 million bbls from January 1981 through October 1981. Record U.S. stockpile purchases of approximately 500,000 b/d, combined with the acceleration of European purchases to take advantage of declining costs, indicate that the aggregate amount in stockpiles may soon exceed 3.5 billion bbls.

Concern about increasing spot-market stockpile purchases at the outbreak of the Iran-Iraq War gave birth to the idea of developing an oil bank. The plan was originally conceived as an EEC initiative. It was hoped, however, that the EEC oil bank would be expanded to include the IEA as a whole. If implemented, participating countries would subscribe a certain percentage of their stocks (equal to approximately ten days of consumption) to a common fund, against which they would have specified drawing rights.

The plan does not call for the physical exchange of stocks, but rather the exchange of certificates entitling the holder to a quantity held in EEC stocks. EEC officials intended the oil bank as a stopgap device to partially cover local shortages, not as a means of covering a major deficit for an extended period of time. The common fund would also be usuable by a country whose stocks fall below ninety days. This would alleviate pressures on the spot market. A country drawing supplies in excess of its subscription would be obligated to reduce domestic demand by a specified amount.

Some of the initial enthusiasm for the oil bank has waned as the feared crisis failed to materialize. The initial shortfall caused by the Iran-Iraq War was almost 4 million barrels per day, a significant amount. Subsequent production increases by other oil producers, abetted by a partial resumption of Iranian and Iraqi output, and declines in IEA demand, avoided a major problem. The current absence of a crisis atmosphere may postpone efforts at developing such an oil fund.

National Stocks

All developed countries have strategic petroleum stocks, but the structure and size of the various national stockpiles vary widely. French strategic stocks are privately held, while in the United States such reserves are in the public domain, and Germany has a mixed-sector approach. Some countries have highly decentralized stocks, with each part of the industry holding government mandated amounts of supply, while others are centralized. Among those states that employ private industry in the national strategic stockpiling scheme, some combine commercial inventories and strategic stocks, some hold the supplies separate, while others combine both approaches.

Stock volumes differ both in absolute magnitude and in size relative to imports and consumption. There also are differences stemming from measurement methods and inaccuracies. Measured in terms of days average net-imports, the major European consuming countries (France, Germany, Italy) and Japan are holding 80 to 90 days of stocks. The United Kingdom, a net exporter, has 90 days of inland consumption. The large refining trade handled by the Netherlands gives the Dutch over 100 days of average net imports because stocks are inflated by refinery inventories. U.S. inventories are a bit less, but averaged 220 days of net imports in 1980. Countries with significant indigenous production relative to consumption, such as Canada, the United Kingdom, and the United States, are the most able to withstand a curb in net imports.

16 International Energy Agency

The Response of Consumers

The industrialized countries were jolted into action about energy supply policy by the rapid changes in the world oil industry in the early 1970s. The success OPEC enjoyed in wresting control of the international oil industry from the major companies was a political and economic defeat for the OECD states. Unilateral OPEC decisions quadrupling prices and setting production levels, punctuated by an OAPEC embargo of the U.S. and selected European markets, reinforced the newly recognized vulnerability of the oil-importing countries.

While EEC members had somewhat coordinated energy policies, the OECD was not prepared for the OPEC price rises. Prompted by Secretary of State Henry Kissinger, in February 1974, thirteen of the twenty-four OECD states convened the Washington Energy Conference. Underlining the urgency of the situation, in November 1974, sixteen OECD members met in Paris and signed the Agreement on an International Energy Program (IEP). Twenty-one OECD states currently are signatories to the IEP.[1] France is the main non-signatory. French participation in EEC energy programs, which are usually complementary to those of the IEP, integrates it into the OECD energy framework regardless of its unwillingness to accede to the IEP.

The IEP created the International Energy Agency, the institution with responsibility for implementing the provisions of the IEP. The main purpose of the IEA is to insure sufficient energy supplies in the event of a supply emergency; accordingly, it seeks to promote access to secure supplies on reasonable and equitable terms and to reduce Western dependence on imported oil. Recognizing the responsibility of government in maintaining an adequate flow of supplies, the IEA envisions an increased government role in home-country petroleum industries and at ongoing consultation between consumer-state governments and the oil firms. The IEA is commissioned to promote cooperation between the industrialized consumer states and both producer countries and non-IEA oil-importing countries, particularly in the Third World.

The underlying premise of the IEA is that well-orchestrated, collective action on the part of the developed countries will prove more effective in countering the power of OPEC and the oil exporting countries of the Third World than would the isolated policies of any single state. The formation of a consumer-nation forum was viewed as necessary not only to express Western interests and to balance the market and political strength of the oil exporters, but also to prevent destructive competition among the importing countries. This fear of competitive bilateralism, by which individual consumer nations pursued special deals with producer countries, was reinforced at the time by the Japanese and French efforts to secure direct purchases of Middle East crude and by the U.S. pursuit of a special relationship with Saudi Arabia. Such competition on the part of the consumers might result in demand pressures pushing prices continuously higher, as each country sought to insure itself of adequate access to crude-oil supplies. The fragmented interests of consumer countries, moreover, would suffer from insufficient bargaining strength in the face of OPEC's power as a commodity producer group.

The Oil-Emergency Management System

To provide for consumer-country emergency self-sufficiency, the IEA adopted a complex policy entailing demand restraint, conservation, alternative energy supplies, and a crisis supply-allocation system. The IEA defines three scenarios under which the emergency plan might be activated:

1. a general crisis, in which IEA countries as a group suffer a supply shortfall of more than 7 percent but less than 12 percent below normal consumption;[2]
2. a general crisis, in which the group shortfall is 12 percent of consumption or more; or
3. a single-nation crisis, in which one country experiences a shoftfall of more than 7 percent of consumption, but the group as a whole does not have a 7 percent shortfall.

In the event of a general crisis, the emergency management system is implemented automatically by a trigger mechanism. Upon the declaration of a finding by the secretariat of a supply shortfall equal to or exceeding 7 percent of group consumption, the emergency plan takes effect. The secretariat's decision can be overriden only by a special-majority vote of at least fifteen members (assuming all members are voting). If one country suffers from a 7 percent shortage, it can request that the secretariat implement the emergency management plan. Should the secretariat make a finding that an emergency situation exists, it recommends implementation of the selective sharing formula. In this situation, a special-majority vote requires the support of at least seventeen of the twenty voting members.

The sharing mechanism to cope with a general supply crisis is based on a complex formula calculating each member's oil supply right and determining whether it has an allocation right or allocation obligation. The allocation right is the amount of oil which a country is entitled to receive from other IEA states under the emergency plan, while the allocation obligation indicates the quantity a member is obligated to distribute to other IEA participants.

If a group shortage is more than 7 percent but less than 12 percent of consumption, each member is to restrict consumption to 93 percent of base-period consumption; if the shortfall exceeds 12 percent, permissible consumption is 90 percent of base-period consumption. Each IEA member is expected to absorb the first 7 percent or 10 percent of the domestic shortfall (depending on the extent of the crisis) by curbing demand. Demand restraint can take the form of conservation measures, rationing, price increases, or any combination of policies.

In effect, although each IEA state would have the same level of permissible consumption, a shortfall would not be equally shared. The formulas are only accounting procedures. A country with substantial shut-in capacity or alternative supplies can use these energy sources to avoid the self-imposed burden of restraining demand or drawing down stocks. Stock drawdowns could also be accelerated to avoid curbing demand. Moreover, because estimated available supplies are based on normal domestic production rather than on current or potential production, a country with rapidly expanding production or a large shut-in capacity will not be forced to shoulder an equal share of the shortfall.

In the event of an individual country suffering from a shortfall in excess of 7 percent, that country is expected to absorb the first 7 percent of the supply deficit by means of demand restraint. The unaffected countries share the shortfall proportionally based on domestic consumption.

The general oil-emergency management plan has never been used. The volatile situation in the Middle East, highlighted by the Iranian Revolution and the Iran-Iraq War prompted concern that a supply crisis might develop. Shortfalls to date have been short-lived, as consuming nations cut their oil demand and other producers increased their crude-oil output. The gravest threat continues to be the potential spread of regional hostilities. Should the vulnerable Straits of Hormuz be blocked or strategic oil fields be shut or wreaked as a result of military operations, a crisis of sufficient magnitude to trigger the general sharing mechanism is a real possibility.

The selective emergency plan also has never been implemented. In May 1979, Sweden petitioned for activation of the selective allocation plan, claiming that the Iranian crisis had precipitated a supply shortage greater than 7 percent of consumption. The secretariat found that the Swedish shortfall was less than 7 percent and the request was denied. Prior to this, only Italy requested employment of the selective emergency sharing system. That request also was denied.

Oil Futures and Supply Crises

The IEA has no official position with respect to the trading of oil futures. The trade in petroleum products futures, like the futures trade in other commodities, operates at the margins of supply and demand. As an adjunct to the world market, futures trading helps in the distribution of supply and price formation and affords a measure of adjustment to international trade. Under normal market conditions petroleum-futures trading is harmonious with the IEA goals of reducing price fluctuations and facilitating distribution.

Petroleum futures are not designed for crisis situations. As the volumes handled by a futures market are marginal, the futures trade often is the first area to feel a supply squeeze. Because these markets are very price sensitive, under crisis conditions contract prices may rise to levels that bear little relation to the larger world market. Crises can trigger direct government involvement in procuring strategic resources, such as oil, and might lead to a suspension of the operations of futures markets.

To employ the closest analogy available, trading on the London Metal Exchange (LME) was suspended during World War II. Prices and supplies were too disrupted to allow hedging or marginal market adjustments. The British government, as part of the war effort, assumed national responsibility for the acquisition, distribution, and stockpiling of strategic metals. In 1939, London banned speculative trading. Controls on foreign exchange, currency flows, and investment further prevented the LME from maintaining operations. Trading was not allowed until a number of years after the war. Copper contracts, which were reinstituted in 1953, were the last to resume trading.

In the event of a supply crisis (as defined by the IEA) the IPE might well suffer a similar fate. National rationing or allocation plans would take precedence over the futures trade. Prices and supplies would exhibit war-time instability and would be subject to government control. Government-controlled prices would remove the need to hedge, destroying the futures trade. IPE product stocks would probably be acquired by the government of either the buyer, seller, or storage facility and integrated into national strategic stocks.

The U.S. petroleum-futures market might be less severely affected. Unlike the IPE, which may have a buyer, seller, and broker from three different countries (while stocks are physically stored in a fourth). U.S. market is characterized largely by domestic transactions. U.S. oil futures, therefore, might be subject to less government control and may be somewhat insulated from the problems of international trade under crisis conditions. Natural supply and price forces, however, would still have an adverse impact on the U.S. futures market. Depending on the nature of a given supply crisis, moreover, the U.S. market may be prey to the same disruptions as the European market, and perhaps even worse.

In short, futures are not a tool for solving major supply problems. A supply crisis would probably result in further restrictions on petroleum futures, perhaps to the point where contract trading was suspended.

Non-Emergency Policies

Politically, the IEA represents the sense of a shared energy future and common interests on the part of the industrialized nations. In many respects it is an analog to the existing economic, political, and strategic links among the OECD states: creating a joint approach to energy issues was a necessary response to the growing importance of energy supply security in international affairs.

On the broadest level, the IEA functions as a permanent forum for conducting the energy discussion. The existence of the agency both guarantees that energy issues will be addressed regularly in a predictable, institutionalized manner and ensures that there will be an appropriate standing body prepared to handle emergencies. This reduces the tendency toward ad hoc responses and policy implementation and discourages separate countries from pursuing individual, uncoordinated policies.

With respect to non-emergency policy areas, the IEA has set a number of medium- and long-term policy goals. National energy programs are required to address a number of problem areas. Joint activities are preferred whenever possible, to encourage Western energy integration, reduce needless duplication, create transnational economies of scale, and allow the sharing of costs. The use of timetables and periodic reviews are encouraged as tools to gauge progress.

Increased investment and focus on technological advances are considered essential. Cooperative ventures in this area are particularly encouraged. Joint research, development, and deployment is needed to further institutionalize a multilateral approach to energy issues. Member governments are to stimulate investment in the energy sectors. Private and public bodies alike are encouraged to cooperate in energy research projects.

Evaluation and Prospects

Judging the effectiveness of any energy management program is often confused with the issue of solving energy problems. The nature of the energy problem, however, entails that it be managed rather than solved. The IEA has not solved the supply problem, but has helped to manage it. Managing a problem means effectively coping with it to minimize destabilizing and harmful side effects, while recognizing that the problem still exists. In the absence of a grand solution, effective management is the only alternative to failure. It is in light of its contribution to the OECD's ability to manage energy problems that the IEA must be judged.

To a large extent, any evaluation is subjective and based on intangibles. It is impossible to measure whether the IEA has moderated price increases, prevented embargoes, stimulated conservation efforts, or reduced oil consumption. These things can be accurately measured only by comparison to what would have happened in the absence of the IEA, and such a comparison is not possible.

Despite this caveat, one can point to successes and failures in IEA policies. Bilateralism is less frequent today than before the formation of the IEA. Conversely, the sense of a common Western energy front is widely accepted as a basic tenet of policy among the OECD states. In 1980-1981, moreover, the IEA helped ease market pressures created by the Iran-Iraq War by helping to coordinate the orderly drawdown of oil stocks. The agency reported that member states withdrew 20 million tonnes (from 460 million tonnes to 440 million tonnes) in the three month period from October 1, 1980, through January 1, 1981, to ameliorate market conditions.

Although the IEA has continually discouraged competitive spot-market purchases by consumer governments and oil companies, the agency failed to moderate spot buying in the wake of the Iranian Revolution. Frenzied purchases in 1979 and early 1980—many of which were for the building of stocks in anticipation of impending shortages and price rises—aggravated the delicate situation which then prevailed on world oil markets. In the interim, prices doubled, as consumers chased supplies at increased prices.

Statistically, a number of gains in the energy situation have been realized since the IEA was created. In 1973-1979, for example, the IEA reports that the member states's:

energy consumption per unit of Gross Domestic Product (GDP) declined 8 percent,

petroleum consumption per unit of GDP declined 11 percent, and

indigenous energy production grew 10 percent.

Oil consumption among the twenty-one decreased 7.5 percent in 1980 and fell another 1-2 percent in 1981. Although the IEA goal of reducing the share of petroleum in total energy consumed to 40 percent in 1990 may not be realized, the agency expects to cut oil consumption to 43 percent of total energy use. This is a significant decline from the 50-55 percent level of petroleum dependency that prevailed in most IEA countries in 1980. Oil imports as a share of total energy consumption, which is currently about one-third, should be reduced to about 27 percent by 1990.

In 1980, the IEA established, for the first time quotas for individual countries to complement aggregate oil-import target levels. By requiring that purchases be registered, the agency hopes to keep close watch on petroleum imports and encourage members to stay within the quota limits. Actual IEA imports in 1980 were under 21 b/d, or more than 10 percent below the agency limit of 23.1 mb/d. The imports targets appear to have been grossly inflated and do not seem to have been a limiting factor. In some respects, the height of the ceilings might have sanctioned additional imports, as some countries may have reasoned that extra purchases were permissible on the grounds that they had not imported their full quota.

For the IEA to remain strong it must continue to meet the needs of the Western countries. The agency has its critics, who say that it acts too slowly, lacks disciplinary power, and is not sufficiently forceful. Moreover, as fears of a general embargo wane, it is increasingly suggested that the emergency management plan—the heart of the IEA—is unnecessary. The failure to activate the emergency allotment plan to treat the shortages that have appeared has prompted other critics to claim that the 7 percent shortfall required to trigger any sharing scheme is excessively high and rigid. In effect, however, this may be a strength. Having never been tested by a real crisis, the emergency management system might be considered the West's ace in the hole that should be reserved for extreme situations.

Proposals, often contradictory in intent, have been made to modify the IEA. While some analysts recommend raising the level of the trigger mechanism higher than 7 percent, others recommend lowering or even abolishing the 7 percent guidepost. Some specialists have claimed that stock levels are too low and do not provide adequate protection. The problem of emergency preparedness is further aggravated by the increasing flow of petroleum outside of the established channels of the Western oil companies. In 1980, the OPEC governments and their national oil companies directly exported more than 50 percent of production. The ability of the IEA to reallocate supplies in the event of a serious shortfall, therefore, has been subject to question.

The fairness of the methods of calculating energy supplies has been questioned. The failure to account for such areas as reserve capacity, alternative fuels, and fuel efficiency raises serious doubts that the burden of a supply disruption would be shared equally.

One of the more interesting and dynamic proposals centers on the notion of developing some type of joint stocks. The idea first emerged at the outbreak of the Iran-Iraq War as a potential response to the risk of spiralling spot prices and a supply shortfall of less than 7 percent. In December 1980, the IEA members agreed in principle to share oil stocks to ensure a balance between oil supply and demand. The idea is based on the development of common stocks, upon which members would have drawing rights (in return for the exercise of which they incur obligations). In a similar vein, Italy has suggested that the IEA should have the authority to allocate all stocks in excess of the ninety-day requirement, or that a certain percentage (5 percent) of the compulsory stocks should be held as a common fund for use by members.

In our opinion, any tendency to downgrade the agency in times of soft prices and abundant supplies, as the world experienced in the 1981–1982 period, should be avoided. Periods of a soft market, on the contrary, should be employed to consolidate the authority and structure of the IEA. In the end, the IEA can be no more effective than the member countries want it to be. It can coordinate only to the extent members cooperate and pursue multilateral goals.

Notes

1. The original signatories of the IEP are Austria, Belgium, Canada, Denmark, Federal Republic of Germany, Ireland, Italy, Japan, Luxembourg, the Netherlands, Spain, Sweden, Switzerland, Turkey, the United Kingdom, and the United States. Since 1974, Australia, Greece, New Zealand, Norway, and Portugal have joined the agreement. Finland, France, and Iceland are the only OECD states that are not parties to the IEP. France is the only EEC member that is not a participant.

2. Normal consumption is calculated as "base period final consumption" (BPFC). The base period is the four quarters previous to the most recently completed quarter, for which it is assumed that complete data is not yet available.

Appendix A
Gas-Oil Prices: Barges, FOB Rotterdam
(U.S. dollars per metric ton)

	January	February	March	April	May	June	July	August	September	October	November	December
1972	26.61	24.02	23.74	25.25	23.92	23.46	24.13	25.68	26.98	28.81	32.43	35.94
1973	37.49	41.88	42.13	43.92	54.71	66.65	72.43	71.39	79.46	121.21	186.52	185.91
1974	131.92	103.49	100.37	83.62	90.54	88.54	92.89	92.28	93.17	92.29	89.94	92.01
1975	87.20	81.68	82.61	88.41	94.56	106.13	99.29	109.48	115.77	117.76	111.71	105.47
1976	103.41	102.95	104.22	105.65	105.16	105.97	104.07	108.30	111.06	109.58	105.91	112.25
1977	116.16	119.33	115.62	117.40	118.50	118.41	119.71	117.27	115.92	116.93	118.06	120.23
1978	117.85	119.63	122.56	126.67	122.64	121.09	122.50	122.69	126.92	133.85	155.50	151.64
1979	194.31	289.16	251.20	265.82	319.93	362.28	356.55	316.88	325.91	330.22	362.45	356.08
1980	344.17	307.24	297.04	318.90	320.95	312.74	305.58	272.45	284.72	300.84	321.42	299.42

Source: Reprinted with permission from *Platt's Oil Price Handbook and Oilmanac*. Copyright McGraw-Hill, Inc. New York: McGraw-Hill, Inc., various years.

Note: Monthly weighted averages computed from the high and low daily average prices.

Appendix B
Low-Sulfur Fuel-Oil
Prices: Barges,
FOB Rotterdam
*(U.S. dollars per
metric ton)*

	January	February	March	April	May	June	July	August	September	October	November	December
1972	13.82	14.85	15.68	15.58	16.97	17.75	17.58	17.25	17.25	17.25	18.03	22.22
1973	24.60	26.59	25.55	24.90	27.49	29.05	26.82	22.87	24.28	30.91	56.00	129.68
1974	115.73	81.53	71.85	66.83	68.83	68.05	65.58	65.58	67.97	71.33	74.65	76.96
1975	81.65	79.64	79.65	77.33	71.74	64.87	62.03	63.81	63.18	61.23	63.84	66.16
1976	68.65	70.93	69.72	69.90	70.37	68.64	69.61	74.85	77.57	77.76	79.51	85.31
1977	90.21	90.94	85.01	83.73	84.44	83.27	83.80	83.56	83.23	84.17	85.20	87.05
1978	86.69	85.71	86.66	87.49	85.04	83.72	82.50	77.14	78.35	89.23	103.89	96.97
1979	111.50	133.25	119.05	125.22	142.01	156.19	155.65	155.45	161.60	173.37	186.60	205.90
1980	196.19	182.88	184.90	182.30	185.97	188.23	187.81	182.29	184.44	205.33	235.00	238.37

Source: Reprinted with permission from *Platt's Oil Price Handbook and Oilmanac*. Copyright McGraw-Hill, Inc. New York: McGraw-Hill, Inc., various years.

Note: Monthly weighted averages computed from the high and low daily average prices.

**Appendix C
High-Sulfur Fuel-Oil
Prices: Barges,
FOB Rotterdam**
*(U.S. dollars per
metric ton)*

	January	February	March	April	May	June	July	August	September	October	November	December
1972	12.75	13.00	14.13	14.13	14.00	13.25	13.63	14.38	14.75	13.75	14.33	14.33
1973	15.60	17.35	19.00	16.60	16.00	17.75	18.35	17.50	15.60	16.25	29.50	75.00
1974	135.00	82.50	77.50	64.50	66.25	65.50	62.75	60.00	63.00	63.25	66.75	70.00
1975	69.75	69.50	70.75	70.75	67.00	63.00	60.75	54.00	59.75	54.00	52.00	57.50
1976	58.75	69.50	66.75	62.75	64.50	64.50	64.50	65.00	68.00	71.25	71.00	72.25
1977	76.00	83.25	76.00	73.75	70.50	71.75	74.60	75.75	75.85	76.60	78.00	77.75
1978	80.25	76.50	75.50	75.50	75.00	73.35	73.35	73.00	70.50	73.00	81.00	81.50
1979	84.05	103.52	106.68	109.87	128.63	142.11	140.65	138.48	139.67	156.20	174.90	178.74
1980	164.17	145.01	143.94	155.13	161.29	153.57	150.00	152.60	162.90	202.42	232.17	219.81

Source: Reprinted with permission from *Platt's Oil Price Handbook and Oilmanac.* Copyright McGraw-Hill, Inc. New York: McGraw-Hill, Inc., various years.

Note: Monthly weighted averages computed from the high and low daily average prices.

Appendix D
Gasoline Prices: Barges, FOB Rotterdam
(U.S. dollars per metric ton)

	January	February	March	April	May	June	July	August	September	October	November	December
1972	23.49	23.78	24.15	25.26	27.78	29.90	31.13	31.97	33.68	35.15	37.72	41.00
1973	45.36	48.82	54.37	63.62	85.36	100.37	93.06	75.40	78.10	92.18	140.54	176.94
1974	144.36	146.34	175.14	171.31	163.98	138.28	115.92	106.13	104.27	100.25	101.54	105.62
1975	108.27	110.00	111.67	117.01	124.66	131.73	120.14	118.43	120.02	122.91	128.19	130.54
1976	127.04	131.46	136.15	141.38	143.41	142.88	140.57	139.29	135.78	137.41	136.04	134.09
1977	132.54	130.56	129.90	134.50	133.63	131.79	131.77	131.70	131.00	131.07	130.73	130.30
1978	129.82	132.41	138.25	137.97	139.72	140.97	147.79	171.28	178.18	190.54	211.49	201.49
1979	208.95	312.36	285.42	298.14	358.97	387.08	366.08	341.52	333.20	345.48	379.80	402.37
1980	389.60	376.36	369.90	362.60	366.11	363.12	351.52	316.63	327.53	345.74	369.32	357.99

Source: Reprinted with permission from *Platt's Oil Price Handbook and Oilmanac*. Copyright McGraw-Hill, Inc. New York: McGraw-Hill, Inc., various years.

Note: Monthly weighted averages computed from the high and low daily average prices.

Appendix E
Futures Contracts: New York Harbor, Heating Oil

150.01   SCOPE
The provisions of these rules shall apply to all No. 2 heating oil and No. 6 industrial fuel oil bought or sold for futures delivery on the Exchange with New York Harbor delivery.

150.02   CONTRACT UNIT
The contract unit shall be 42,000 U.S. gallons (1,000 U.S. barrels). The seller shall deliver not less than 39,900 U.S. gallons (950 U.S. barrels) nor more than 44,100 U.S. gallons (1,050 U.S. barrels), except that if delivery is made by book transfer pursuant to Rule 150.04(A)(3), the seller shall deliver 42,000 U.S. gallons (1,000 U.S. barrels). The volume delivered shall be determined at 60°F using A.S.T.M. Standard D1250, Table 6 B.

150.03   GRADE AND QUALITY SPECIFICATIONS
The oil shall be a hydrocarbon oil free from alkali, mineral acid, grit, fibrous or other foreign matter and shall meet the following physical and chemical properties:

(A) Heating Oil—sometimes known as No. 2 Heating oil
(1) Gravity: A.P.I. (American Petroleum Institute) 30° minimum (A.S.T.M. Test Method D287)
(2) Flash: 130°F minimum (A.S.T.M. Test Method D93)
(3) Viscosity: Kinematic, Centistokes at 100°F, minimum 2.0, maximum 3.6 (A.S.T.M. Test Method D445)
(4) Water and Sediment: 0.05% maximum (A.S.T.M. Test Method D1796 or D2709)
(5) Pour Point: 0°F maximum (A.S.T.M. Test Method D97)
(6) Distillation: 10% Point, 480°F maximum; 90% Point, 640°F maximum, End Point 670°F maximum (A.S.T.M. Test Method D86)
(7) Sulfur: 0.20% maximum (A.S.T.M. Test Method D129 or D1552)
(8) Color: maximum 2.5 (A.S.T.M. Test Method D1500)

(B) Industrial Fuel Oil—sometimes known as No. 6 residual oil
(1) Gravity: A.P.I. (American Petroleum Institute) 10° minimum, 30° maximum (A.S.T.M. Test Method D287)
(2) Flash: 150°F minimum (A.S.T.M. Test Method D93)
(3) Viscosity: S.S.U. (Saybolt Seconds Universal) at 100°F, 50 seconds minimum, 6000 seconds maximum (or comparable results using Saybolt Seconds Furol or Kinematic (A.S.T.M. Test Method D88 or D445)

This contract, which became effective as of October 29, 1982, has been abridged and reprinted with permission of the New York Mercantile Exchange.

(4) Water and Sediment: 1% maximum (A.S.T.M. Test Method D95 and D473, or D1796)

(5) Pour Point: 60°F maximum (A.S.T.M. Test Method D97)

(6) Sulfur: 0.30% maximum (A.S.T.M. Test Method D129 or D1552)

NOTE: (A.S.T.M. = American Society for Testing Materials)

150.04   DELIVERY

(A) Delivery shall be made F.O.B. seller's New York Harbor ex-shore facility with all duties, entitlements, taxes, fees and other charges imposed prior to delivery on or in respect to the product paid by the seller. At buyer's option, such delivery shall be made by any of the following methods which are applicable:

(1) By delivery into buyer's barge or truck;

(2) By delivery into buyer's tanker or pipeline, if buyer can take delivery in such manner at the facility used by seller;

(3) By stock transfer of title to the buyer, if the facility used by seller allows such transfer, or by book transfer if the seller agrees to such transfer;

(4) By intra-facility transfer ("pump-over"), if the facility used by seller allows such transfer;

(5) By inter-facility transfer ("pump-over"), if the facilities used by seller and buyer both allow such transfer.

For the purpose of these rules, New York Harbor shall extend from the East River west of Hunts Point; Gowanus Bay west of the Hamilton Avenue Bridge; the Hudson River south of the George Washington Bridge; the Upper Bay; the Narrows; the Lower Bay west of Norton Point; the Newark Bay; the Hackensack River and Passaic River south of the Pulaski Skyway Bridge; the Kill Van Kull; the Arthur Kill and the Raritan River east of the Garden State Parkway Bridge.

(B) If delivery is taken by truck the buyer shall pay a per gallon surcharge in such amount as is published by the Exchange each month 15 business days prior to the close of trading. The surcharge shall be determined in the following manner:

Based on prices quoted in the weekly PAD I Report of the Oil Price Information Service, truck differentials will be derived for that week for each company which has listed both No. 2 reseller barge and No. 2 truck rack prices. The differential shall be the difference between a company's barge price and a mean of both its New York City and Newark truck rack prices, provided, however, that where a truck price is quoted for only one location, that price alone will be used in the calculation. The highest and lowest truck differentials so established will be omitted and the mean for that week will be calculated based on the remaining differentials. The truck surcharge published by the Exchange will be a mean of the four most recently available weekly mean differentials.

(C) All deliveries made in accordance with these rules shall be final and there shall be no appeal.

Appendix F
Futures Contracts: Gulf
Coast, Heating Oil

170.01   SCOPE
The provisions of these rules shall apply to all No. 2 Heating Oil
bought or sold for future delivery on the Exchange with Gulf Coast
delivery.

170.02   CONTRACT UNIT
The contract unit shall be 42,000 U.S. gallons (1,000 U.S. barrels). The seller shall deliver not less than 39,900 U.S. gallons (950
U.S. barrels) nor more than 44,100 U.S. gallons (1,050 U.S. barrels),
except that if delivery is made by book transfer pursuant to Rule
170.04(A)(3), the seller shall deliver 42,000 U.S. gallons (1,000 U.S.
barrels). The volume delivered shall be determined at 60°F using
A.S.T.M. Standard D1250, Table 6 unabridged.

170.03   GRADE AND QUALITY SPECIFICATIONS
The oil delivered shall be a hydrocarbon oil free from alkali,
mineral acid, grit, fibrous or other foreign matter, meeting the re-
quirements of the Colonial Pipeline Company (Atlanta, Georgia) for
fungible fuel oil—40 cetane (FGX-76-Northern Grade) then in effect,
and shall meet the following physical and chemical properties:
(A) Gravity: A.P.I. (American Petroleum Institute) 30° mini-
mum (A.S.T.M. Test Method D287)
(B) Flash: 130°F minimum (A.S.T.M. Test Method D93)
(C) Water and Sediment: 0.05% maximum (A.S.T.M. Test
Method D1796 or D2709)
(D) Pour Point: 0°F maximum (A.S.T.M. Test Method D97)
(E) Sulfur: 0.20% maximum (A.S.T.M. Test Method D129 or
D1552)
(F) Color: maximum 2.5 (A.S.T.M. Test Method D1500)
(G) Viscosity: Kinematic, Centistokes at 100°F, minimum 2.0,
maximum 3.6 (A.S.T.M. Test Method D445)
(H) Distillation: 10% Point, 480°F maximum; 90% Point,
640°F maximum, End Point 670° maximum (A.S.T.M. Test Method
D86)

170.04   DELIVERY
(A) Delivery shall be made F.O.B. seller's Gulf Coast ex-shore
facility having access to any Colonial Pipeline injection point with all
duties, entitlements, taxes, fees and other charges imposed prior to
delivery on or in respect to the product paid by the seller. At buyer's
option, such delivery shall be made by any of the following methods
which are applicable:

This contract, which became effective as of September 24, 1981, has been abridged and reprinted with permission of the New York Mercantile Exchange.

(1) By delivery into buyer's barge, tanker or the Colonial Pipeline;

(2) By delivery into other pipelines, if buyer can take delivery in such manner at the facility used by the seller;

(3) By transfer of title to the buyer without physical movement of product ("book transfer"), if the facility used by seller allows such transfer;

(4) By intra-facility transfer ("pump-over"), if the facility used by the seller allows such transfer;

(5) By inter-facility transfer ("pump-over"), if the facilities used by seller and buyer both allow such transfer.

(6) By truck, if the facility used by the seller allows such transfer.

For the purpose of these rules, Gulf Coast shall extend from Pasadena, Harris County, Texas to Collins, Covington County Mississippi, and include facilities located in Brazoria County, Texas and Jackson County, Mississippi which have access to Colonial Pipeline injection points in Pasadena, Texas and Collins, Mississippi.

(B) If delivery is taken by truck and buyer shall pay $.005 per gallon surcharge. All other deliveries shall be at par except for Colonial Pipeline deliveries at Beaumont (Jefferson County, Texas), Port Arthur (Jefferson County, Texas), Lake Charles (Calcasieu Parish, Louisiana), Baton Rouge Junction (E. Feliciana Parish, Louisiana) or Collins (Covington County, Mississippi). Such deliveries shall be at a differential reflecting the rates and charges which apply to the transportation of Petroleum Products as described in and subject to the provisions of ICC 29, supplements thereto, or reissues thereof, issued by Colonial Pipeline Company, from and to the points named herein.

(C) All deliveries made in accordance with these rules shall be final and their shall be no appeal.

Appendix G
Futures Contracts: New York Harbor, Gasoline

NOTE: These Rules apply to two separate petroleum product futures contracts: One for delivery of leaded regular gasoline, and one for delivery of unleaded regular gasoline. The terms and conditions of these two contracts are identical in all respects except with regard to (Rule 190.03) *Grade and Quality Specifications.* Subsection (A) of Rule 190.03 is applicable only to the unleaded regular gasoline contract. Subsection (B) of Rule 190.03 is applicable only to the leaded regular gasoline contract.

190.01   SCOPE
          The provisions of these rules shall apply to all leaded regular gasoline and unleaded regular gasoline bought or sold for future delivery on the Exchange with New York Harbor delivery.

190.02   CONTRACT UNIT
          The contract unit shall be 42,000 U.S. gallons (1,000 U.S. barrels). The seller shall deliver not less than 39,900 U.S. gallons (950 U.S. barrels) nor more than 44,100 U.S. gallons (1,050 U.S. barrels), except that if delivery is made by book transfer pursuant to Rule 190.04(A)(3), the seller shall deliver 42,000 U.S. gallons (1,000 barrels). The volume delivered shall be determined at 60°F using A.S.T.M. Standard D1250, Table 6 B.

190.03   GRADE AND QUALITY SPECIFICATIONS
          The oil shall be a hydrocarbon oil free from alkali, mineral acid, grit, fibrous or other foreign matter and shall meet the following physical and chemical properties:
          (A) Unleaded regular gasoline
          (1) Gravity: A.P.I. (American Petroleum Institute) 52° minimum (A.S.T.M. Test Method D287)
          (2) Color: undyed
          (3) Corrosion: 3 hours at 122°F, maximum 1 (A.S.T.M. Test Method D130)
          (4) Lead: maximum 0.03 grams per gallon (A.S.T.M. Test Method D2599 or equivalent)
          (5) Doctor: negative (A.S.T.M. Test Method D484) or, if necessary, Mercaptan Sulfur: weight percent, maximum 10 parts per million (A.S.T.M. Test Method D3227)
          (6) Octane: RON minimum 91.0 (A.S.T.M. Test Method D2699); MON minimum 82.0 (A.S.T.M. Test Method D2700); (RON & MON)/2 minimum 87.0, (RON & MON)/2 maximum less than 91.0.

This contract, which became effective as of October 29, 1982, has been abridged and reprinted with permission of the New York Mercantile Exchange.

(7) Reid Vapor Pressure: maximum pounds, January — 14.5, February — 14.5, March — 13.5, April — 13.5, May — 11.5, June 10, July — 10, August — 10, September — 11.5, October — 13.5, November — 13.5, December — 14.5 (A.S.T.M. Test Method D323)

(8) Distillation:

Northern Grade	Class
December, January, February	E
March, April, October, November	D
May, September	C
June, July, August	B

	B	C	D	E
10% evaporation °F maximum	149	140	131	122
50% evaporation °F minimum	170	170	170	170
50% evaporation °F maximum	245	240	235	230
90% evaporation °F maximum	374	365	365	365
End Point °F maximum	430	430	430	430

(A.S.T.M. Test Method D86)

(B) Leaded regular gasoline

(1) Gravity: A.P.I. (American Petroleum Institute) 52° minimum (A.S.T.M. Test Method D287)

(2) Color: yellow or bronze in sufficient quantity to meet United States Surgeon General's minimum requirements

(3) Corrosion: 3 hours at 122°F, maximum 1 (A.S.T.M. Test Method D130)

(4) Lead: maximum 4.00 grams per gallon (A.S.T.M. Test Method D3341 or equivalent)

(5) Doctor: negative (A.S.T.M. Test Method D484) or, if necessary, Mercaptan Sulfur: weight percent, maximum 10 parts per million (A.S.T.M. Test Method D3227)

(6) Octane: RON report (A.S.T.M. Test Method D2699); MON report (A.S.T.M. Test Method D2700; (RON + MON)/2 minimum 89.0

(7) Reid Vapor Pressure: maximum pounds, January — 14.5, February — 14.5, March — 13.5, April — 13.5, May — 11.5, June — 10, July — 10, August — 10, September — 11.5, October — 13.5, November — 13.5, December — 14.5 (A.S.T.M. Test Method D323)

(8) Distillation:

Northern Grade	Class
December, January, February	E
March, April, October, November	D
May, September	C
June, July, August	B

	B	C	D	E
10% evaporation °F maximum	149	140	131	122
50% evaporation °F minimum	170	170	170	170

	B	C	D	E
50% evaporation °F maximum	245	240	235	230
90% evaporation °F maximum	374	365	365	365
End Point °F maximum	430	430	430	430

(A.S.T.M. Test Method D86)

190.04   DELIVERY

(A) Delivery shall be made F.O.B. seller's New York Harbor ex-shore facility with all duties, entitlements, taxes, fees and other charges imposed prior to or as a result of delivery paid by the seller. Delivery shall be made in accordance with applicable Federal, State and local laws. Buyer shall reimburse seller for any gasoline tax as had been or will be paid by the seller. At buyer's option, such delivery shall be made by any of the following methods which are applicable:

(1) By delivery into buyer's barge or truck;

(2) By delivery into buyer's tanker or pipeline, if buyer can take delivery in such manner at the facility used by seller;

(3) By stock transfer of title to the buyer, if the facility used by seller allows such transfer, or by book transfer if the seller agrees to such transfer;

(4) By intra-facility transfer ("pump-over"), if the facility used by seller allows such transfer;

(5) By inter-facility transfer ("pump-over"), if the facilities used by seller and buyer both allow such transfer.

For the purpose of these rules, New York Harbor shall extend from the East River west of Hunts Point; Gowanus Bay west of the Hamilton Avenue Bridge; the Hudson River south of George Washington Bridge; the Upper Bay; the Narrows; the Lower Bay west of Norton Point; the Newark Bay; the Hackensack River and Passaic River south of the Pulaski Skyway Bridge; the Kill Van Kull; the Arthur Kill and the Raritan River east of the Garden State Parkway Bridge.

(B) If delivery is taken by truck the buyer shall pay $.0025 (.25¢) per gallon surcharge.

(C) All deliveries made in accordance with these rules shall be final and there shall be no appeal.

190.05   PETROLEUM COMMITTEE

The Board of Governors shall appoint a Petroleum Committee whose duty it shall be to advise the Board with respect to the futures contracts traded under these rules.

190.06   DELIVERY MONTHS

Trading may be conducted in contracts providing for delivery in 18 consecutive calendar months commencing with the current calendar month, subject to the requirement that the listing of each such month for trading be submitted to the Commission in accordance with the provisions of Section 5a(12) of the Commodity Exchange Act and the Commission's regulations thereunder. The Board of

Governors or the Clearing House Committee shall determine the day on which trading in a delivery month commences.

190.07   PRICES AND FLUCTUATIONS
(A) Prices shall be quoted in dollars and cents per gallon. The minimum price fluctuation shall be $.0001 (.01¢) per gallon. The maximum permissible price fluctuation in any one day shall be $.02 (2¢) per gallon above or below the preceding day's settling price (the "basic maximum fluctuation").

(B) If the settling price for any month shall move by the basic maximum fluctuation in either direction, the maximum permissible fluctuation in either direction for all months during the next business session shall be 50% above the basic maximum fluctuation.

(C) If the settling price for any month for a business session for which the maximum permissible fluctuation is 50% above the basic maximum fluctuation shall not move by said expanded maximum permissible fluctuation in either direction, the maximum permissible fluctuation for all months during the next business session shall be the basic maximum fluctuation.

(D) If the settling price for any month for a business session for which the maximum permissible fluctuation is 50% above the basic maximum fluctuation shall move by said expanded maximum permissible fluctuation in either direction, the maximum permissible fluctuation in either direction for all months during the next business session shall be twice the basic maximum fluctuation.

(E) The expanded maximum permissible fluctuation established in accordance with section (D) above shall remain in effect for all subsequent business sessions until the business session next following the first session at which the settling price for no month shall move by said expanded maximum permissible fluctuation in either direction. At such next business session the maximum permissible fluctuation in either direction for all months shall be 50% above the basic maximum fluctuation.

(F) There shall be no maximum limit on price fluctuations during the month preceding the delivery month.

190.08   TERMINATION OF TRADING
Trading in the current delivery month shall cease on the last business day of the month preceding the delivery month.

190.08A   PRODUCT PLACEMENT
For purposes of Rule 54.02, a Clearing Member (seller) will be deemed to be in a position to fulfill his contractual obligation on a maturing contract if, prior to one hour before the time established for the beginning of the closing range of the applicable delivery month, such seller has received from his customer a certification in the form prescribed by the Exchange stating that the customer has or will have in position, not later than the calendar day following the fifth business day of the delivery month, at one or more eligible delivery facilities at which delivery may be made in accordance with this Chapter, the quantity and quality of oil sufficient to meet such

customer's contractual obligations to make delivery when and as prescribed in these Rules; provided, however, that the receipt of such certification shall not relieve the seller of any obligations under any Rules other than Rule 54.02.

190.09   DELIVERY PROCEDURE
           (A) CLEARING MEMBERS HAVING OPEN LONG POSITIONS (BUYERS)
           (1) By 12:00 o'clock noon on the first business day of the delivery month, a buyer having an open long position shall file with the Exchange a properly completed and signed Notice of Intention to Accept. The Notice of Intention to Accept shall be on the form prescribed by the Exchange and shall include the names of the buyer's customers, the number of contracts and such additional information as may be required by the Exchange. The buyer may, at its option, request in the Notice of Intention to Accept a preferred delivery site, but such request shall not be binding upon the seller.
           (2) As soon as possible after receipt from the Exchange of a Delivery notice, but not later than 4:30 p.m. on a business day which shall be not later than the fourth business day of the delivery month, the buyer shall give to the seller identified in such Delivery Notice, with a copy to the Exchange, properly completed and signed Initial Delivery Instructions, on the form prescribed by the Exchange, which shall include the following information and such additional information as may be required by the Exchange:
           (a) Name of seller
           (b) Tender Number
           (c) Name and Location of Delivery Facility specified in the Delivery Notice.
           (d) Number of Contracts
           (e) Method of Delivery
           (f) A consecutive five day period for initiation of delivery.
     The buyer shall verify with the seller, prior to giving the seller Initial Delivery Instructions, that the method of delivery specified therein conforms to the normal capabilities of such facility with respect to the manner and time of delivery and the quantity to be delivered. Initial Delivery Instructions may not be amended after they have been given to the seller.
           (3) Not later than 10:30 a.m. on a business day at least one business day following the giving of Initial Delivery Instructions and at least two calendar days prior to the time of the proposed delivery, which time must be within the consecutive five day period set forth in the buyer's Initial Delivery Instructions, the buyer shall give to the seller, with a copy to the Exchange, properly completed and signed Delivery Instructions on the form prescribed by the Exchange, which shall include the following information and such additional information as may be required by the Exchange.
           (a) Name of seller
           (b) Tender Number
           (c) Name and Location of Delivery Facility specified in the Delivery Notice

(d) Number of Contracts

(e) Method of Delivery (which must conform to the normal capabilities of the facility named in the Delivery Notice with respect to the manner and time of delivery and the quantity to be delivered)

(f) Name of proposed Carrier (i.e., Barge, Truck, Tanker or Pipeline), and the approximate size of the barge, truck, or tanker, if any

(g) For interfacility transfers, name of receiving facility

(h) Date and Approximate Time for Initiating Delivery

Delivery Instructions given after 10:30 a.m. on any day shall be deemed to have been given on the following business day. Delivery Instructions may not be amended after they have been given to the seller.

(4) (a) If the buyer receives from the seller a Notice of Clearance advising that the seller will deliver pursuant to the Delivery Instructions, the buyer shall require its customer to post with it the full purchase price of all product to be purchased under all contracts covered by such Notice less any margin already on deposit for such contracts, on a business day at least two days prior to the scheduled initiation of delivery.

(b) If the buyer receives from the seller a Notice of Non-Clearance advising that it is unable to deliver in accordance with the Delivery Instructions, it shall give to the seller, no later than 10:30 a.m. on the third business day following receipt of such Notice, with a copy to the Exchange, revised Delivery Instructions in accordance with the provisions of sub-paragraph (3) above and shall thereafter comply with the provisions of this sub-paragraph (4) as if such revised Delivery Instructions were the original Delivery Instructions. Such revised Delivery Instructions shall specify a delivery date and time not less than 24 hours before or after the delivery time specified in the original Delivery Instructions (whether or not such date and time is within the five-day period specified in the Initial Delivery Instructions), provided such date and time is prior to the last business day of the delivery month and at least two calendar days subsequent to the date on which such revised Delivery Instructions are given to the seller. Revised delivery instructions given after 10:30 a.m. on any day shall be deemed to have been given on the following business day. Revised Delivery Instructions may not be amended after they have been given to the seller.

(B) CLEARING MEMBERS HAVING OPEN SHORT POSITIONS (SELLERS)

(1) By 12:00 o'clock noon on the first business day of the delivery month, a seller having an open short position shall file with the Exchange a properly completed and signed Delivery Notice. The Delivery Notice shall be on the form prescribed by the Exchange and shall include the names of the seller's customers, the name and location of the facility which will supply the product, the number of contracts and such additional information as may be required by the Exchange.

(2) Not later than 4:30 p.m. of a day on which the buyer gives the seller Delivery Instructions, the seller shall give the buyer a properly completed and signed Notice of Clearance on the form prescribed by the Exchange, with a copy to the Exchange, indicating that it is prepared to make delivery in accordance with the provisions of the buyer's Delivery Instructions. Delivery Instructions given after 10:30 a.m. on any day shall be deemed to have been given on the following business day. In the event that the seller is unable to make delivery in accordance with the buyer's Delivery Instructions because of a bona fide inability to receive clearance from the facility, the seller shall, not later than 4:30 p.m. of the day on which the buyer gives the seller Delivery Instructions, give to the buyer a Notice of Non-Clearance, with a copy to the Exchange, and state the reasons for such inability. The seller may, at its option, in the Notice of Non-Clearance suggest on alternate delivery site and/or a preferred delivery date or time. If Notice of Non-Clearance is given, the seller shall require its customer to post, at the time the Notice of Non-Clearance is given, additional original margin equal to 25% of the total contract value of all contracts listed in the Delivery Instructions. Such additional margin shall be posted by the seller with the Exchange not later than 11 a.m. on the next business day.

(3) Not later than 4:30 p.m. of the day on which the buyer gives the seller revised Delivery Instructions, the seller shall give the buyer a Notice of Clearance, with a copy to the Exchange, indicating that it is prepared to make delivery in accordance with the provisions of the buyer's revised Delivery Instructions. Revised Delivery Instructions given after 10:30 a.m. on any day shall be deemed to have been given on the following business day. In the event that the seller is unable to make delivery in accordance with the buyer's revised Delivery Instructions because of force majeure, the seller shall, not later than 4:30 p.m. of the day on which the buyer gives the seller revised Delivery Instructions, give to the buyer a Notice of Non-Clearance with a copy to the Exchange, and state the reasons for such inability. If Notice of Non-Clearance is given pursuant to this subparagraph, the delivery covered by such Notice will be referred to the Petroleum Delivery Committee no later than the next business day.

(C) Settling Price: The last settling price shall be the basis for delivery.

(D) Notice Day: The Clearing House shall allocate Delivery Notices and Notices of Intention to Accept by matching size of positions to the extent possible. The Clearing House shall pass copies of the notices to the respective Clearing Members on the morning of the next business day prior to the opening of trading. The day the notices are passed to the Clearing Members shall be referred to as the Notice Day. There shall be only one Notice Day, which shall be the second business day of the delivery month.

(E) Non-Transferable: The Clearing Member who receives a Delivery Notice or a Notice of Intention to Accept from the Clearing House shall be deemed to have agreed to accept or deliver product. Delivery Notices or Notices of Intention to Accept are not transferable.

(F) Delivery Day:

(1) All deliveries must be completed after the fifth business day and before the last business day of the delivery month.

(2) Shipment will commence when product passes the buyer's cargo intake flange, tank or pipeline connection, at which point the buyer shall assume the risk of loss.

(3) The buyer shall pay the seller at the office of the seller by certified check by 12:00 noon of the business day following the receipt of the product. Amount of payment shall be based on volume delivered as determined at 60°F using A.S.T.M. Standard D1250, Table 6 B. Should the Exchange approved inspector be unable to supply quantitative results prior to the time established in the Rules for payment of the product, amount of payment shall be based initially on 42,000 U.S. gallons per contract. Payment adjustments based on actual quantity transferred shall be completed between Clearing Members by 12:00 noon of the third business day after transfer of product.

(a) If the buyer requires multiple delivery dates (i.e., truck delivery), multiple payments shall be required for each portion of product transferred.

(b) The seller upon receipt of payment shall give the buyer a bill of lading or other quantitative certificate and all appropriate documents that may be necessary to transfer ownership of the product to the buyer.

(4) The day the buyer receives the stated product shall be referred to as the Delivery Day.

(5) The foregoing notwithstanding, if, at any time during the delivery month:

(i) a seller who has received revised Delivery Instructions notifies the Petroleum Delivery Committee that delivery at the time and/or site designated may not be accomplished because of force majeure, or

(ii) a buyer who has received a Notice of Clearance but prior to delivery notifies the Petroleum Delivery Committee that circumstances constituting force majeure prevent acceptance of delivery at the time and/or site designated.

(6) The Petroleum Delivery Committee, based upon such information as may be furnished to it by the buyer and the seller and as may otherwise be obtained by it, shall determine whether force majeure exists and may (i) order an extension of time for delivery up to five days from the scheduled time, provided, however, that any such extended delivery shall be completed not later than the fifth business day of the calendar month following the delivery month, and/or (ii) change a delivery site provided that the seller has product at the new site or will have product there in time for delivery, and/or (iii) modify the method of taking delivery if such method is acceptable to the buyer, and/or (iv) allocate deliveries. The Petroleum Delivery Committee shall confer with the buyer and the seller prior to issuing any order under this Section, and shall notify the buyer and the seller of its determination within two business days of notification hereunder which may be after the time

nominated for delivery. Thereafter, the delivery procedure will be completed as otherwise provided in this Chapter. In exercising its authority under this Section, the Petroleum Delivery Committee may not require a site or method of delivery other than provided in Rule 190.04. The Petroleum Delivery Committee's order shall be deemed final and may not be appealed. If the buyer or the seller claims that the circumstances leading to an order of the Petroleum Delivery Committee under this Section were caused by the action of the seller or the buyer, respectively, the party asserting such claim, after complying with the Petroleum Delivery Committee's order, may submit a claim in arbitration, pursuant to Rule 51.05, against the other party.

190.10   SHIPMENT
          (A) The seller's ex-shore facility must have a minimum draft of 20 feet at mean low water and a minimum access draft of 20 feet at mean low water. The seller must supply the product as soon as the barge or tanker reports readiness to load, or if delivery is to be made on shore, to supply the product as soon as the buyer reports the transfer facility or truck is ready to accept the product.
          (B) The buyer must accept the product after the fifth business day and before the last business day of the delivery month. The buyer's barge or tanker must be safely afloat at all times.
          (C) The seller shall pay all applicable demurage charges if his shore facility is unable to deliver the product at a rate sufficient to meet normal requirements for loading a barge or tanker or to deliver ex-tank or pipeline at a normal rate. The buyer shall pay all other demurrage charges.

190.11   VALIDITY OF DOCUMENTS
          The Exchange makes no representation respecting the authenticity, validity or accuracy of any inspection certificate, Delivery Notice, Notice of Intention to Accept, bill of lading, check or of any document or instrument delivered pursuant to these rules.

190.12   INSPECTION
          (A) The buyer shall notify the seller in writing not later than 4:30 p.m. on a business day which shall be not later than the fourth business day of the delivery month, that a grade and quality and/or quantity inspection(s) is requested at place of delivery. The buyer may request the tests for any or all grade and quality specifications for the stated product listed in Rule 190.03. The buyer may request a quantity inspection for all deliveries and is required to request a quantity inspection for delivery by barge, tanker or interfacility transfer (pump-over).
          (B) If a buyer requests grade and quality and/or quantity inspection(s), the buyer shall appoint an Exchange approved inspector. If the buyer does not request a quantity inspection, the seller may request such inspection and shall appoint an Exchange approved inspector.

(C) If the product meets grade and quality specifications, the buyer and seller shall share equally in the cost of inspection. If the product does not meet grade and quality specifications, the seller shall pay the cost of inspection. The cost of verifying the quantity of product transferred shall be shared equally by buyer and seller.

(D) The Exchange approved inspector shall determine the quantity of product transferred by using the prevailing practice of the ex-shore facility transferring the product.

190.13   TRADING IN SPREADS

A spread shall consist of the simultaneous purchase of one future month and sale of another future month at a stated price difference. The purchase and the sale shall be for one account. Floor brokers executing spreads shall properly record them in writing so as to permit the identification of the transactions and the parties thereto. All spread trading on this Exchange must be made by open outcry. All spread trading must be in line with current spread differentials. Both months must be within the trading range of the day at the time of execution, provided, however, that where one month or both months are then at the permissible trading limits of the day, one month shall be priced within the actual trading range of the day at the time of execution and the other month shall be priced within the permissible trading limits of the day. The seller in each contract must report on a pit card the spread price and differential to the Floor Supervisor. Spread transactions shall be recorded on special spread sales panels. The Exchange ticker shall record and publish a spread differential only. Spread transactions shall not set off stops in any contract except for spread stops.

190.14   EXCHANGE OF FUTURES IN CONNECTION WITH CASH COMMODITY TRANSACTIONS OR FUTURES FOR CASH COMMODITIES

(A) An exchange of futures in connection with cash commodity transactions or futures for cash commodities is permitted before 11:00 a.m. of the first business day following termination of trading in a future contract. No such exchange shall be made by a seller who does not, at the time of such exchange, have in his possession, or have a binding commitment from a responsible third party to deliver, a cash commodity which is a petroleum product, and no such exchange shall be made which does not require delivery of such cash commodity within a reasonable period of time.

(B) A report of such exchange shall be submitted to the Exchange which report shall identify the exchange as made under this Rule and shall contain the following information: a statement that the exchange has resulted in a change of ownership and the date thereof, the kind and quantity of the cash commodity, the kind and quantity of the futures, the price at which the futures transaction is to be cleared, the names of the clearing members and such other information as the Exchange may require. Each buyer and seller involved in such exchange must satisfy the Exchange, at its request, that the transaction is bona fide. All documentary evidence relating to the exchange, including, without limitation, evidence as to change of ownership and possession by the seller of the cash commodity or commitment therefor shall be obtained and retained by the buyer and seller for examination by the Exchange for such length of time as is prescribed for various books and records by Section 1.31 of the Regulations of the Commodity Futures Trading Commission.

(C) The report of such exchange shall be given, and notice thereof shall be posted on the floor of the Exchange, on the day that the agreement with respect thereto was entered into, or if such agreement was entered into after the close of trading, then on the next business day. Such exchanges shall be cleared through the Exchange in accordance with normal procedures, shall be clearly identified as exchange transactions and recorded as such by the Exchange and by the Clearing Members involved.

190.14A   ALTERNATIVE DELIVERY PROCEDURE
A seller or buyer may agree with the buyer or seller with which it has been matched by the Exchange to make and take delivery under terms or conditions which differ from the terms and conditions prescribed by this Chapter. In such a case, the buyer and seller shall execute an Alternative Delivery Notice on the form prescribed by the Exchange and shall deliver a completed, executed copy of such Notice to the Exchange. The delivery of an executed Alternative Delivery Notice to the Exchange shall release the buyer, the seller, and the Exchange from their respective obligations under the Exchange contracts involved. In executing such Notice, the buyer and seller shall indemnify the Exchange against any liability, cost or expense it may incur for any reason as a result of the execution, delivery, or performance of such contracts or such agreement, or any breach thereof or default thereunder. Upon receipt of an executed Alternative Delivery Notice, the Exchange will return to the buyer and seller all margin monies held for the account of each with respect to the contracts involved.

190.15   LATE PERFORMANCE AND FAILURE TO PERFORM
(A) Late Performance
(1) Failure to Comply with Rules Constituting Late Performance
(a) Unless otherwise provided by the Rules, a seller or buyer shall be late in performance if it fails to perform an obligation relating to delivery or payment within the time established in accordance with the provisions of these Rules.
(b) A seller or buyer who is late in performance, and who does not perform the obligation with respect to which it is late in performance within five days of such late performance, shall, unless otherwise provided by the Rules, have failed to perform and may no longer perform such obligation; provided, however, that a buyer who has failed to make a payment shall make such payment.
(2) Charges for Late Performance
(a) A seller or buyer who is late in performance shall pay to the other party $100.00 per contract for each day of late

performance, not exceeding five days. The Exchange shall bill the seller or buyer who is late in performance for such charges and, when collected, shall remit them to the other party.

(b) A seller or buyer who is late in performance shall pay to the Exchange a charge equal to 10% of the contract value for each contract for each day of late performance not exceeding five days.

(c) Any charge imposed pursuant to subparagraph (a) or (b) may be waived or reduced by the Board of Governors if it shall determine that the late performance was due to force majeure or that there are other mitigating circumstances which justify such waiver or reduction.

(3) Disciplinary Proceedings for Late Performance

The imposition of the charges for late performance set forth in this Chapter shall be governed by the provisions of this Chapter and shall be independent of the Rules governing disciplinary proceedings. Late performance shall be deemed a violation of the Rules and shall be subject to the provisions of Rules governing disciplinary proceedings, provided, however, that no fine, in addition to the charges provided for in this Rule, shall be imposed in any disciplinary proceeding solely by reason of a late performance referred to in this Rule.

(B) Failure to Perform

(1) A seller or buyer shall, unless otherwise provided by the Rules, fail to perform if it is late in performance pursuant to these rules, and does not perform the obligation with respect to which he is late in performance within five days of such late performance.

(2) Failure to Perform

The seller or the buyer which fails to perform shall pay to the other party, as liquidated damages in lieu of all other damages, including consequential damages, 10% of the contract value for each contract which has not been performed. The Exchange shall bill the party which has failed to perform for such liquidated damages and, when collected, shall remit them to the other party. Payment of damages for failure to perform shall be in addition to any other payments due from the seller or the buyer to the other party pursuant to this Chapter.

(3) Disciplinary Proceedings for Failure to Perform

A failure to perform shall be deemed a violation of the Rules and shall be subject to the Rules governing disciplinary proceedings, provided, however, that no fine, in addition to the charges payable to the Exchange provided for in this Chapter, shall be imposed in any disciplinary proceeding solely by reason of a failure to perform referred to in this Rule.

(C) Definitions

As used in this Chapter:

(1) The term "contract value" shall mean the value of the contract computed on the basis of the last settling price for the delivery month.

(2) The term "other party" shall mean the corresponding buyer(s) where the seller is late in performance or has failed to perform, and the corresponding seller(s) where the buyer is late in performance or has failed to perform.

(3) The term "day of late performance" and variations thereof shall mean a business day in the case of a late performance with respect to an obligation which can, pursuant to the Rules, be performed on a business day only and a calendar day in the case of a late performance with respect to an obligation which can, pursuant to the rules, be performed on a non-business day as well as a business day. The first day of a late performance shall be the day following the last day on which a party may perform his obligation under the Rules without being late in performance. The day on which a party who is late in performance subsequently performs his obligations under the rules is a day of late performance, provided, however, that a party may not perform such obligation except an obligation to make payment after it has failed to perform.

(4) The term "force majeure" shall mean any circumstances (including but not limited to a strike, lockout, national emergency, governmental action, or act of God) which is beyond the control of such buyer or seller, and which prevents the buyer or seller from making or taking delivery of product when and as provided for in this Chapter.

190.16   MARGINS

(A) All margins shall be recommended by the Clearing House Committee and approved by the Board of Governors except as provided in (B) below and may be changed from time to time.

(1) Clearing Member's margins shall be deposited with the Clearing House.

(2) Customer's margins may be equal to but not less than Clearing Member's margins and shall be deposited with the Clearing Member.

(3) A straddle margin shall be required on a straddle transaction. When one side of the straddle is undone, the remaining side shall carry regular margin requirements.

(B) Additional margins may be required of each Clearing Member and each customer on all open trades in such futures and in such amount as the President may deem necessary.

(C) Maintenance Margins

When the customer's margins are impaired to the extent of 30%, they must be restored to the initial amount required by the foregoing, except that if the requirement at prevailing prices varies from that required when the trades were initiated, either the margin originally deposited or the prevailing margin rate, whichever is lower, may be used as the basis for calculation of the point at which restoration is necessary. Equities in accounts may be withdrawn only to the extent that such equities exceed the margin requirements at the prevailing level.

(D) Penalties for Failure to Deposit Margins

Additional margin or the replenishment of original or additional margin may be demanded by carrying broker on and during any business day when debits (exclusive of commissions) so require. Any customer who, for any reason, fails to respond to a call from his carrying broker to deposit required margin will confer upon the broker the right to close out all or such part of the open trades of such customer as will leave any remaining unliquidated contracts fully margined, and the customer shall be liable for any loss or deficiency resulting therefrom. The customer's response to a margin call from his broker must be full and complete. Failure of the broker to receive such margin in readily available U.S. funds, within a reasonable time, or to be notified that margin has been sent, shall require the carrying broker, without prejudice to his interest, to liquidate or reduce the account or accounts involved to a fully margined basis.

190.17   REFERENCES TO SELLER AND BUYER

References in these rules to the "seller" and "buyer" shall mean the short Clearing Member and the long Clearing Member respectively.

Appendix H
Futures Contracts: Gulf Coast, Crude Oil

Salient Features

Unit of Trading	1,000 barrels (42,000 gallons) per contract.
Price Basis	FOB the Capline System in St. James, Louisiana or FOB seller's designated port facility in either St. James, St. John the Baptist, St. Charles, Jefferson, Orleans, St. Bernard and Plaquemines Parishes, Louisiana. Prices quoted in dollars and cents per barrel.
Delivery Options	Buyer shall choose a pipeline delivery (at the Capline System in St. James, Louisiana) or a non-pipeline delivery (at the seller's designated port facility). Non-pipeline deliveries shall be into buyer's barge or tanker or by any of the following methods, if seller's designated facility allows: into shoreside tankage, by "pump-over" or by "book-transfer."
Delivery Instrument	Wet barrels.
Standards	Origin: Domestic crude petroleum produced in Southern Louisiana, crude petroleum from the LOOP's Segregation Number 1, or foreign crude petroleum with one of the following stream designations: Bonny light, Brass River, Ekofisk, Escravos, Qua Iboe, Saharan blend, and Zarzaitine. Sulfur (by weight): .50% maximum. Gravity (API at $60°F$): $35.0°$ minimum. Pour Point: $55°$ maximum for summer and $30°$ maximum for other months. Viscosity: 325 SUS at $60°F$ maximum. Reid Vapor Pressure: 9.5 p.s.i. at $100°F$ maximum. Water and Sediment (by volume): 1% maximum.

This contract, which became effective as of July 22, 1982, has been abridged and reprinted with permission of the Chicago Board of Trade.

Quality Differentials	Two (2) cents per barrel premium per degree, or fraction thereof, above 35° and up to 40°.
Maximum Daily Price Move	100 cents per barrel ($1,000.00 per contract).
Minimum Daily Price Move	1 cent per barrel ($10 per contract).

Appendix I
Futures Contracts: Gulf Coast, Propane

Basis of Contract	1,000 barrels (42,000 gallons) of propane meeting the specifications set forth in NGPA-HD-5 (NGPA Publication 2140-68 or any revision thereto).
Trading Hours	9:45 a.m.–2:35 p.m. (New York Time) Monday–Friday
Cash Market Trading	12 noon–1:00 p.m. (New York Time) Delivery made in accord with Exchange Rules within five (5) business days.
Trading Months	The current delivery month and the eleven succeeding months.
Price Quotations and Price Fluctuations	Propane is quoted in cents per gallon as for example 40.25 or 40 and 25/100 cents per gallon. The minimum daily price fluctuation is 1/100 of a cent, called a "point." The maximum daily price fluctuation is 300 points above or below the previous trading session's settling price for each trading month. A point, 1/100 of a cent, represents $4.20 on a 1,000 barrel contract.
Last Trading Day	At 2:35 p.m., on the last business day prior to the notice day for the delivery month.
Notice Day	There is only one notice day which shall be the fifth business day prior to the delivery day.
Delivery Day	The first business day of the delivery month.
Delivery Points	A) Mont Belvieu, Texas (Near Houston) The current licensed facilities are: 1) Coastal States Marketing, Inc. 2) Texas Eastern Transmission Corp.

This contract has been abridged and reprinted with permission of the New York Cotton Exchange.

B) Group 145, Conway, Kansas

The currently licensed facility is Mapco Underground Storage, Inc.

Delivery is at the seller's option. The deliverer at Group 145 (Conway, Kansas) will make an allowance to the receiver equal to the tariff per gallon of the published commercial pipeline tariff rates between Conway and Mont Belvieu. The pipelines involved are the Mid-America Pipeline from Conway, Kansas to Hobbs Station, Texas, and the Seminole Pipeline from Hobbs Station to Mont Belvieu, Texas.

Although the delivery point is at the option of the seller, buyers who receive product at Group 145 may arrange to actually take delivery in Mont Belvieu. The licensed facilities have a working agreement in effect which facilitates this transfer. A copy of this agreement is on page 11.

Delivery Procedure

All trades are cleared through members of the Commodity Clearing Corp., the clearing house associated with the Petroleum Associates of the New York Cotton Exchange, Inc. The clearing house acts as a buyer to every seller and a seller to every buyer, and as a guarantor of contract performance by its members. It also facilitates the transfer of funds between its members which results from trading activity.

Delivery is handled by the Member Firms through the Commodity Clearing Corp.

The delivery day in propane is the first business day of the delivery month.

On the 6th business day prior to the delivery day, a non-transferable notice is presented by the seller's member firm to the Commodity Clearing Corp., not later than one hour after the close of the market.

The notice is issued prior to the opening of the market on the following morning to the buyer's member firm. Notice day is the fifth business day prior to the delivery day. The notice price is filled in by the Commodity Clearing Corp., on behalf of the issuer of the notice.

The member firm must remind its (seller) customer that it must make propane available in the licensed facility prior to the delivery day and obtain a shipping certificate from the licensed facility. This shipping certificate must be registered with the Exchange prior to the delivery day.

Invoicing and Delivery of Documents

The deliverer (Clearing Member) shall tender to the receiver (Clearing Member) before 2:00 p.m. (New York Time) on the day of delivery. The shipping certificate and other documents required the By-Laws and Rules of the Exchange.

An invoice for the Liquefied Propane Gas stating the location of the licensed facility at which the delivery shall be made, and with adjustment for any credits or allowances required in accordance with the By-Laws and Rules of the Exchange shall be rendered to the buyer (Clearing Member) before 11:00 a.m. (New York Time) on the day of delivery.

The receiver (Clearing Member) shall at that time make payment to the deliverer by a certified check, which unless mutually agreed upon, must be drawn on a New York Bank, in the amount called for by the deliverer's (Clearing Member) invoice. The member receiving the delivery will then return the Notice of Delivery to the issuer.

Delivery of a Liquefied Propane Gas contract shall be made at the settlement price established by the Commodity Clearing Corporation on the day previous to the day the Notice is issued.

Notices

Are not transferable. A member receiving such a notice is obligated to accept delivery in accordance with the By-Laws and Rules of the Exchange.

Delivery notices must be presented to the Commodity Clearing Corporation not later than one (1) hour after the close of the market on the day preceding the date of issuance.

Notices will be delivered prior to the opening of trading in propane on the date of issuance.

Delivery Method

A shipping certificate, issued by one of the licensed facilities. The presentation of the shipping certificate to the licensed facility allows the receiver to take possession of his propane. The certificate expires on the last day of the delivery month.

Terms and Conditions

The charge for the preparation and issuance of the certificate and the storage for the delivery month is paid by the seller. Contact your brokerage firm or the Exchange for the current fee.

The buyer must provide the licensed facility within five (5) calendar days after receiving the shipping certificate with instructions as to the final disposition of the product at the end of the storage period.

The licensed facilities agree to deliver propane for shipment within 21 calendar days from the date of demand by the holder of the certificate.

In the event of the failure of a certificate holder to exercise its privileges on or before its expiration date, the licensed facility reserves the right to sell or dispose of the propane and after taking compensation for all charges due on the product will remit the remainder to the holder.

Appendix J
Commodity-Futures
Markets and Products,
United States and
United Kingdom

United States

ABT
    American Board of Trade: Canadian dollar (Can $), British pound (Brit £), German mark (DM), Swiss franc (SF), yen, U.S. Treasury bills, gold bullion, silver bullion, silver coins, platinum, copper, plywood

ACEX
    American Commodity Exchange: (GNMA Certs) Government National Mortgage Association Certificates, ninety-day U.S. Treasury Bills

CBT
    Chicago Board of Trade: silver, long-term U.S. Treasury Bonds, four–six-year U.S. Treasury notes; GNMA Certs, certificates of deposit, wheat, corn, soybeans, soybean oil, soybean meal, iced broilers, commercial paper (thirty- and ninety-day), oats, plywood, No. 2 oil

CME
    Chicago Mercantile Exchange: boneless beef, live cattle, feeder cattle, live hogs, pork bellies, skinned hams, butter, fresh eggs, frozen eggs, nest run eggs, plywood, random length lumber, stud lumber, russet potatoes, milo, turkeys, fresh broilers, SF, Mexican Peso (MP), DM, Can $, Brit £, yen, French franc (FF), Dutch guilder (DG), gold, copper; U.S. silver coins, domestic certificates of deposits, ninety-day U.S. Treasury bills; one-year U.S. Treasury bills; four-year U.S. Treasury notes

CSCE
    Coffee, Sugar, and Cocoa Exchange: coffee, sugar, cocoa

COMEX
    Commodity Exchange, Incorporated: silver, copper, gold; ninety-day U.S. Treasury bills; two-Year U.S. Treasury notes, GNMA Certs

IMM
    International Monetary Market (a division of CME): gold, Brit £, Can $, DM, yen, SF, DG, FF, copper, MP, U.S. silver coins, ninety-day U.S. Treasury bills, one-Year U.S. Treasury bills,

four–six-year U.S. Treasury notes, eurodollar deposits, certificates of deposit

KCBT   *Kansas City Board of Trade:* wheat, Value Line stock index

MIDAM   *Mid-American Commodity Exchange:* wheat, corn, oats, soybeans, silver, U.S. silver coins, gold, live cattle, live hogs

MINEX   *Minneapolis Grain Exchange:* wheat

NOCEX   *New Orleans Commodity Exchange:* Cotton, rough rice, milled rice

NYCEX   *New York Cotton Exchange:* cotton, orange juice, wool, propane, crude-oil (inactive)

NYFE   *New York Futures Exchange* (a division of the New York Stock Exchange): long-term U.S. Treasury bonds, ninety-day domestic-bank certificates of deposit

NYMEX   *New York Mercantile Exchange:* platinum, potatoes, No. 2 oil, No. 6 industrial oil (inactive), leaded and unleaded regular gasoline, imported lean beef, palladium

United Kingdom

IPE   *International Petroleum Exchange:* gas oil

LCE   *London Commodity Exchange:*
              CTM   The Coffee Terminal Market: coffee
              GAFTA   The Grain and Feed Trade Association: barley, wheat
              LCT   The London Cocoa Terminal Market: cocoa
              LRT   The London Rubber Terminal Market: rubber
              LVT   The London Vegetable Oil Terminal Market: vegetable oil, soy oil
              LWT   The London Wool Terminal Market: wool
              SOMFA   The Soybean Meal Futures Association: soybean meal
              UTS   The United Terminal Sugar Market: sugar No. 2, sugar No. 4

LME   *London Metal Exchange:* aluminum, copper cathodes, copper wirebars, lead, nickel, silver, tin (high and low grades), zinc

LPFA   *London Potato Futures Association:* potatoes

Index

About the Contributors

Albert L. Danielsen is professor of economics at the University of Georgia. He received the B.S. from Clemson University in 1960 and the Ph.D. from Duke University in 1966. He recently authored a book entitled *The Evolution of OPEC* and has written numerous articles and research reports on energy markets. He has also served in the U.S. Department of Energy as special assistant to the deputy assistant secretary for International Energy Research.

Kenneth Potter, a chartered mechanical engineer, has been active in the oil industry since 1946 when he joined the Texas Oil Company. In 1960 he moved to Conoco, Inc., and in 1981 retired as director of marketing to become an energy consultant. A founding member of the United Kingdom Liquefied Petroleum Gas Industry Technical Association, he has also served as its chairman. Mr. Potter has represented the United Kingdom on the Bureau of the European Liquefied Petroleum Gas Association (AEGPL–Paris) and recently completed a two-year term as its president.

About the Authors

William G. Prast is president of Atlantis, Inc., a consulting firm that specializes in energy and mineral economics. Before establishing Atlantis, he served for fifteen years in the international-operations and government-affairs departments of a large energy company, Conoco Inc. Dr. Prast is a member of the Society of Petroleum Engineers of the American Institute of Mining, Metallurgical and Petroleum Engineers (AIME), the American Economic Association, and the Royal Institution of Mining and Metallurgy, London; and a fellow of the Institute of Petroleum, London. His many publications include *Securing U.S. Energy Supplies* (Lexington Books, 1981). He received the B.S. and M.S. in petroleum and natural-gas engineering and the Ph.D. in mineral economics from The Pennsylvania State University.

Howard L. Lax was manager of policy analysis for Atlantis, where he directed the research and writing of studies that address political and economic issues in energy and minerals. Mr. Lax has published papers and books on the international oil and minerals industries. He is a Ph.D. candidate in political science at the City University of New York and teaches political science at Queens College.